THE AUTHOR

Ian A. McLaren trained as a secondary school teacher and taught in secondary schools in New Zealand and London. He spent a year (1953-54) as an Imperial Relations Trust Fellow at the University of London Institute of Education, and was awarded the Fulbright Travel Grant to the University of Chicago (1957-58). Dr McLaren has lectured in New Zealand: in History at Palmerston North Teachers' College (1956-59), and in Education at the Victoria University of Wellington (1960-71). Since 1972, he has been Professor of Education in the University of Waikato, Hamilton, New Zealand.

WORLD EDUCATION SERIES

Education in a Small Democracy: New Zealand

World education series

GENERAL EDITOR: DR BRIAN HOLMES
Reader in Comparative Education
Institute of Education
University of London

Education and Development in Latin America
Laurence Gale

Education in Communist China
R. F. Price

Reforms and Restraints in Modern French Education
W. R. Fraser

Education in a Small Democracy: New Zealand

IAN A. McLAREN
University of Waikato, New Zealand

ROUTLEDGE & KEGAN PAUL
London and Boston

First published in 1974
by Routledge & Kegan Paul Ltd
Broadway House, 68–74 Carter Lane,
London EC4V 5EL and
9 Park Street,
Boston, Mass. 02108, U.S.A.
Printed in Great Britain by
Richard Clay (The Chaucer Press), Ltd,
Bungay, Suffolk

ISBN 0 7100 7798 X

Library of Congress Catalog Card No. 73-91035

Contents

Contents

Part Two: Major Social Issues

Part Three: Educational Problems

Contents

Illustrations

Acknowledgments

I am indebted to my colleagues, Professor C. L. Bailey, Mr J. L. Ewing and Mr H. Hayden of the Department of Education, and Dr A. D. Robinson, of the School of Political Science and Public Administration, the Victoria University of Wellington, for the encouragement and assistance they gave me during the writing of this book. I wish to record my thanks also to officers of the national Department of Education and to the staff of the New Zealand Council for Educational Research for information and assistance generously given; to Dr L. Weidner of the Pädagogische Hochschule Heidelberg, Professor G. Baron of the Institute of Education, University of London and Professor J. F. Kerr of the University of Leicester for their helpful comments on a draft manuscript; to Dr B. Holmes in particular for his skilful editing and guidance in the methodology of comparative education; to Miss P. Hendle, Mrs A. Haw and Miss C. Macdonald for their care in typing not always very legible manuscripts and to my wife for her always constructive criticism of my literary efforts. Those named are not, of course, in any way responsible for the accuracy of the text or for errors of judgment.

World education series

The volumes in the World Education Series will treat national systems of education and, where appropriate, features of different systems within a particular region. These studies are intended to meet the needs of students of comparative education in university departments and schools of education and colleges of education and will supplement the growing volume of literature in the field. They may also appeal to a wider lay audience interested in education abroad.

As an area study of a national system each volume presents an accurate, reasonably up-to-date account of the most important features of the educational system described. Among these are the ways in which the school system is controlled, financed and administered. Some account is given of the various kinds of school within the system and the characteristics of each of them. The principles of curriculum organization and some aspects of teacher education are outlined. Of more interest, however, is the analysis which is made in each volume of the unique national characteristics of an educational system, seen in the context of its history and the sociological, economic and political factors which have in the past and continue now to influence educational policy.

The assumption behind the series is, however, that common socio-economic and educational problems find unique expression in a particular country or region, and that a brief analysis of some major national issues will reveal similarities and differences. Thus, while in each case the interpretation of policies and practices is based on the politics of education, the interpretative emphasis will vary from one country to another.

The framework of analysis for each volume is consequently the same, attention being drawn in the first section to the legal basis of educational provision, followed in the second section by an analysis of the political considerations which have and do influence the formulation, adoption and implementation of policy. The role of political parties is described where appropriate and the influence of the church or churches on policy examined. Attention too is given to the activities of pressure groups at national, regional and local levels. Changing industrial, urban and familial patterns are used to show how educational needs are in process of change and what difficulties arise when innovations are attempted. Again, each author touches on the extent to which economic resources affect the implementation of policy. The analysis relates principally to the twenty-year period between 1945 and 1965 but relevant aspects of the pre-Second World War period are described and the chains of events are seen in historical perspective.

Finally, in the third section some account is given of problems which arise within the educational system itself. Those which appear to the author of particular interest and importance have been treated in some depth. Others have been referred to so that readers may consult other sources of information if they wish. Broad problem areas in education have, however, been identified. The points of transition within a system between the first and second and between the second and third stages of education give rise to problems of selection and allocation. Under conditions of expansion, created by explosions of population and aspirations, traditional solutions are often thought to be no longer adequate. The attempts made to meet these new situations are described. So too are the relationships and debates about them, between the various types of school at different levels of education. For example what are the possibilities of transfer between academic, general and technical/ vocation schools at the second stage of education? And where these different types have been replaced by some form of common or comprehensive school what kinds of differentiation exist within the single school? At the third level of higher education what relationships exist between institutions providing general education, professional training and research opportunities? In some systems a form of dual control is growing up with the universities retaining much of their traditional autonomy and the technological institutes and teacher education institutions increasingly feeling the influence of government agencies. Again, after a process of differentiation in course content in the first stage of higher education there is now a tendency for the first year (or two) of college or university work to be regarded as a preparatory year (or years) with common or somewhat similar courses of studies for all students.

Particular attention has been paid to the problems which arise in the area of teacher education. Movements in most countries are in the direction of bringing together the previously separate systems of training for elementary and secondary school teachers. Common entrance prerequisites to different training institutions may now be required. Where this is not yet the case training colleges usually make it possible for students to obtain, during the course of their studies, a certificate which grants entry to the university and highest (in prestige and status) forms of teacher education. The place of teacher education in the structure of higher education is, in short, discussed in each of the volumes. So are debates about curricular content and methods of certification.

Finally, some attention is given to the interaction of the schools and other social agencies. Among these the health services, youth organizations, the family, the Church, industry and commerce have been regarded as important. Where special note is not taken of such institutions the impact they have in the schools is dealt with throughout the volume as a whole.

The framework in short is intended to facilitate cross cultural studies through the series as a whole. Basic educational legislation is referred to in the belief that it gives the most reliable and valid source of national goals or aims in education. The problems of putting these into effective action are socio-economic-political and educational. Comparisons can be made, therefore, between the aims of education as expressed in national legislation and between the main factors which inhibit or facilitate practical provisions in accordance with these aims.

BRIAN HOLMES
General Editor

General editor's introduction

New Zealand is a small country but it is renowned at least in Britain for its dairy produce, mutton and lamb, its middle distance runners, its rugby footballers, the fighting qualities of its young men in time of war and the efforts it has made to create a just multi-racial society. As a result of the legislation passed by the Liberal Government which came to power in 1891 New Zealand won world fame as a country which introduced advanced social services while still only on the threshold of economic development. The growth of educational provision, accelerated when the Labour Party came to power in 1935, reflects this. For example in 1936 free post-primary education was made available to young people up to the age of nineteen. Ian McLaren's thesis in this account of education in New Zealand is that the commitment made in 1939 by the Minister of Education in a Labour Government has been endorsed by all subsequent administrations. The problems of development have not been created by deep ideological differences but have been a consequence of changes in society and constraints inherent in the educational system itself.

Solutions have been sought within a tradition that is British—a blend of English and Scottish influences dating effectively from the nineteenth century when in 1840, after a period of uncertainty, the Union Jack was hoisted. In 1852 New Zealand was granted self-government and by 1856 had a full parliamentary system based upon provincial councils which were abolished in 1876 so that control effectively passed to Parliament. In spite of regional and local participation in education the central Department of Education has in New Zealand been able, since 1914, to exercise real control. This contrasts sharply with the relative weakness in England and Wales of the central authority until fairly recently. The creation of a Ministry of Education (now the Department of Education and Science) by the 1944 Education Act has allowed for the slow accumulation of power by the Central Government in England and Wales. In New Zealand centralized power is effectively in the hands of the administrators in the Department of Education who are, of course, responsible to the minister. Although he has always held Cabinet rank the latter's position is politically rather weak. Education is not a portfolio sought by an ambitious politician. Within the Cabinet its status is low and it has not in post-war administrations been seen as a stepping stone to a more senior appointment. The convention that education should not be the subject of party political debate reduces the opportunity a politician has to demonstrate his political skills. The non-controversial commitment to free education for all as a human right and to the idea of equality of educational provision inevitably takes educational policy out of the party political arena and makes it a matter of debate among educationists, i.e. administrators and teachers.

The absence in New Zealand of an aristocracy of birth or wealth and a much less rigid worker–management structure makes the provision of equal educational facilities much less dependent than in England and Wales on social class background. Status is more a matter of a person's level of education and professional position. And in such a society the prestige and status-power conferring function of private, fee-paying schools, are not nearly so great as in Britain.

Some problems, growing out of this tradition, persist. What role should the churches play in education? As in England denominational struggles to control education preceded attempts by the churches to ensure that some form of religious instruction was provided in the state schools and to obtain financial aid. The solution in New Zealand ran along different lines. The 1877 Education Bill included a clause, repeated in the 1914 and 1964 Education Acts, which ensured that teaching in state primary schools would be secular. Religious instruction in the secondary schools is at the discretion of the controlling authorities. As for finance the creation of a dual system along the lines established in England and Wales was deliberately rejected. The 1877 Bill rejected any form of financial or administrative partnership between church and state in the field of public education. The Protestants allowed their schools to become part of the public system, the Roman Catholics, in New Zealand as elsewhere, built up their own system of primary schools so that by 1969 three-quarters of the private primary schools in the country were Catholic. The issue of aid, raised repeatedly by the Catholic authorities, has persisted in the post-Second World War period. In the 1960s more money was made available to private schools. Rivalries between Catholic and Protestant groups gave way to co-operation in attempts to gain more support and it seems likely that in a less acrimonious climate of opinion non-state schools will receive more money from the government.

Other long-standing problems have exercised the attention of the Department of Education since 1945. The needs of rural children have never been easily met in a country where many children live in outlying districts beyond walking distance of a school. Others live on high country farms, in lighthouses, beside remote bays or in roadless fiords. Buses bring the first group of children to centrally located schools. A Correspondence School meets the needs of children living beyond the reach of the school bus and those who are unable through illness or physical handicap to attend school. These services ensure an equality of provision at the primary level unmatched in most countries of the world. Such solutions are less effective at the secondary level where rural schooling is more limited and contributes to the drift away from the countryside to the urban areas.

The education of Maori children is linked with this issue. Nearly 50 per cent of them still attend country schools but the movement of Maoris into the urban centres in search of work has added new dimensions to a problem which goes back to 1816 when the missionaries first established a school for them. The attitudes of white New Zealanders have varied over the years: sympathy during the late nineteenth century for a dying race of people; tolerance when the number of Maoris rose sharply but they continued to live in remote districts; some hostility during the economic depression of the 1930s; while today policy emphasizes the distinct contribution the Maori people can make to the general life of the country and is directed towards providing them with educational facilities which will meet their particular needs.

To these long-standing problems, have been added those which have arisen since the Second World War because of the population expansion. There were 27,000 births in 1933, 39,000 in 1945, 50,000 in 1946 and 56,000 in 1955. Building programmes frequently failed to keep pace with demands for additional accommodation. The shortage of primary school teachers was acute during the 1950s, the staffing of secondary schools constitutes a problem even in the 1970s. Teacher shortages in the 1950s and 1960s are a world-wide phenomenon. The reasons for them are similar. Ian McLaren analyses the special features of the conditions in New Zealand and describes attempts made there to meet the problems of recruiting, training and retaining teachers.

Again the growth of urban areas and the decline of the old inner core within them have in New Zealand, as elsewhere, created educational problems. The inner city schools, as in England, Australia and the USA, are old, poorly equipped and unattractive to teachers. Frequently most of the children in one of these schools are recent immigrants: in New Zealand from the Pacific Islands or from Europe. The need for special aid to ensure that children living in underprivileged city areas receive equal educational opportunities is recognized. The possibilities of meeting these needs if not as remote as in some of the world's conurbations, are nevertheless not tremendously great even in New Zealand.

In the light of these problems solutions have been adopted designed to provide equal educational provision. Some of the constraints working against the success of such policies lie within the educational system itself. The supply of teachers has been mentioned, but reforms in the structure of the system and in the internal organization of schools have not been easily achieved in spite of government pressure and the power of the central administration. Curricula have changed rather slowly. These lags in education are by no means confined to New Zealand. McLaren reveals some of the reasons for the slowness of educational response while at the same time makes clear the achievements of the system.

The lessons which can be learned from the account of education in a small democracy are revealing. Clearly centralized power is not antithetical to democratic control; church–state relationships, so long a major issue in education, are not incapable of amicable resolution; the existence of a sizeable minority group identifiable in terms of skin colour and cultural background need not lead to insuperable difficulties of equal provision, alienation or the absorption of the minority by the majority; and it is possible, even in countries where many children live in remote districts, to match educational provisions in rural areas with those in the favoured small towns and city suburbs. One thing is clear from Ian McLaren's analysis, fundamental to the success of proposed solutions to the problems of providing a free and equal education are the attitudes of the people who in their various ways implement policy. New Zealanders may well feel proud of their achievements in the field of education.

BRIAN HOLMES

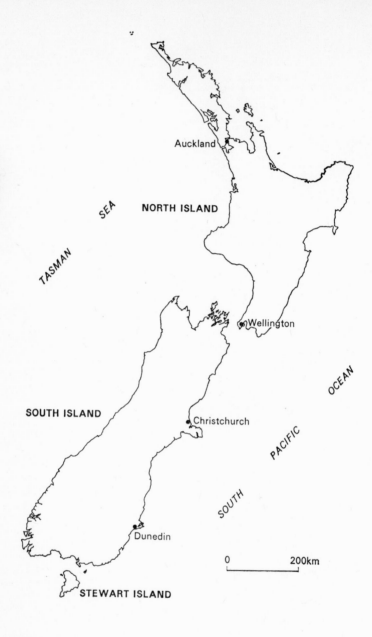

Auckland

NORTH ISLAND

TASMAN SEA

Wellington

SOUTH ISLAND

Christchurch

PACIFIC OCEAN

SOUTH

Dunedin

0   200km

STEWART ISLAND

PART ONE

The politics of education

Principles of policy and administrative control

In 1939, Peter Fraser, Minister of Education in New Zealand's first Labour Government, declared that it was his administration's objective to ensure 'that every person, whatever his level of academic ability, whether he be rich or poor, whether he live in town or country, has a right, as a citizen, to a free education of the kind for which he is best fitted and to the fullest extent of his powers' (*A to J*,*1939, E–1, 2–3).

Both in urban and in rural areas a marked characteristic of New Zealand society has been and is its strongly egalitarian nature. Since the 1890s a common purpose has been to absorb all classes into a doctrineless middle class, content for the most part to achieve only a comfortable mediocrity. Education accordingly has emphasized the production of a high average at the expense of the exceptional. Class distinctions, while undoubtedly existing, are much less rigidly defined than in the United Kingdom. Terms such as 'social ladder' and 'class structure' cannot, without substantial qualification, be applied to New Zealand, where one level of society shades imperceptibly into the next. On the other hand, while inherited status, privilege or wealth is resented, social status is certainly attached to a number of professions. Even so, entry to such favoured occupations (the medical profession ranks highest in popular esteem) depends, in theory at least, only on intelligence and a determination to qualify.

No post-war Minister of Education has ever hinted that his government does not wholly endorse Peter Fraser's 1939 objective. A remark made during a debate on the 1964 Education Bill underlined its complete acceptance by all shades of political opinion: 'All Governments of this country—and there is nothing party political about this—have set out to provide equality of opportunity, especially in education,' claimed an opposing National member (*NZPD*,† 1964, vol. 341, 4033). The same conclusion had been

* *Appendices to the Journals of the House of Representatives.*
† *New Zealand Parliamentary Debates.*

reached two years earlier by the Commission on Education in New Zealand (1962, 11–12):

> Nothing that has been said or written in evidence has given any grounds for believing that there is in the community any large body of sentiment opposed to the ideas expressed by Mr Fraser, nor . . . has there been any movement—social or political—which would suggest any retreat from his viewpoint. Rather it might be claimed that the influence of the Second World War and its aftermath have strengthened this sentiment.

Nevertheless, since 1945 successive governments in pursuit of this ideal have been confronted with a range of problems, some of them apparently intractable. The special needs of rural children in New Zealand have of course long been recognized. The complexities of helping parents who wish to educate their children in private or denominational schools within a secular state system of education have led to heated debate. The education of the indigenous Polynesians, the Maoris, continues to be a matter of particular concern. But other post-war problems could hardly have been suspected in 1939. For example the magnitude of the immediate post-war population explosion and the sustained high level of population growth during the 1950s took education officials completely by surprise as did the massive movement of population away from the rural areas into urban centres.

These problems, the education of rural children, the provision of public support for private (including denominational) schools, concern for Maori education and the difficulties faced by schools in the new urban areas must therefore be seen against a post-1945 population explosion which created new crises within the system, distracting attention from long-standing and major issues.

How in these circumstances has New Zealand attempted to achieve the widely accepted educational goal of equality of opportunity? What significant factors and priority decisions have influenced policy?

The role of the politician

First of all it must be said that unlike some Western European countries, where fundamental theoretical and ideological differences divide national political parties and where there is a tendency for educational discussion to be channelled through them (Holmes, 1967), in New Zealand neither of the principal political parties is fettered by strong ideological bonds. Both are opportunist. Party differences about education are rather of attitudes than of values, of means rather than of ends.

Traditionally, in New Zealand as elsewhere, the Labour Party is believed to be more sympathetic towards education than its opposition. The lustre imparted by the educational achievements of the Labour Government in the late 1930s has not lost its sheen. 'There is not anything,' said the first Labour prime minister, Michael Savage, 'that is too good for the children.' The human right argument still carries more weight in Labour Party than in National Party circles, which stress the need to obtain a profitable return on money invested in education. 'What the tax-payer wants today, and what he demands, is that his money be wisely spent,' asserted a National Government spokesman on education (*NZPD*, 1969, vol. 364, 3845).

Continuing differences in outlook were reflected in the policies of the two principal political parties during the 1969 general election campaign, a campaign in which education was much discussed. Whereas the Labour Party broke new ground in a number of respects, including a highly contentious proposal to assist independent schools, the ruling National Party stood firmly on its past record; National candidates soft-pedalled on all education topics and simply followed the lead of the prime minister in pointing to the substantial increase in educational spending since 1960 when National became the government. What they conveniently overlooked was that these increases were largely forced by inflation, devaluation and the 25 per cent rise in enrolments during their nine years in office. Indeed it might be concluded that the longer any government is in office the more it loses educational momentum. This is not surprising. Politicians themselves are not particularly education conscious (between 1890 and 1971 only one prime minister was a university graduate and he held office only for a fortnight) and the public generally is apathetic. Perhaps both politicians and the majority of the electorate have appreciated that there is little causal relationship between affluence and academic attainment in New Zealand.

This lack of sustained educational debate is also fostered by the convention that education must be kept out of politics. 'I deplore any suggestion of making education the football of politics,' announced one senior politician during the debate on the Department of Education estimates in 1969 (*NZPD*, vol. 364, 3856). As a result 'a conspiracy of silence' seems to have developed in parliament between Labour and National on the subject. Debates on education lack any real depth. They are mainly about specific local problems and local schools, for the New Zealand member of parliament must never forget the immediate needs of his constituency. Although the presentation to parliament of the department's annual estimates affords members an excellent chance to debate broad educational principles and issues, this opportunity is seldom taken.

A measure of parliament's interest in education may be gauged by the fact that while the 1964 Education Bill was before the House there were only eleven principal speakers to it. Even the topic which engenders most heat, namely the question of state financial assistance to independent schools, is usually adroitly side-stepped by the politicians. Yet so long as education enters politics only as an electioneering carrot—a new intermediate school, a gymnasium for a secondary school, and, if the electorate is especially marginal, a teachers' college or even a university—neither parliament nor the political parties can offer the country real educational leadership. New Zealand's eighty-seven members of parliament are extremely busy men and women who are always at the beck and call of their constituents; they have little time or even opportunity to become familiar with basic educational issues and problems and, unfortunately, neither party has the educational expertise available to it which, in British politics, is provided by, for example, the Fabian Society and the Bow Group.

Real progress in education, especially long-term planned development, will be possible in New Zealand only when a government is prepared to re-allocate its resources so that education gets a significantly greater share of them than is the case at present. If, in a proudly proclaimed welfare state, allocations to other services cannot be reduced significantly, the government's only course of action will be to increase general taxation. No government, however, will take either course unless it is convinced that it is politically expedient. This is unlikely while education remains outside party politics, and is the concern mainly of cautious administrators and a few educational interest groups whose members are, like the administrators, dedicated to preserving the present delicate balance within the system. The determination of everyone to keep education out of politics and the absence of deep-rooted ideological differences between the two principal political parties, has meant that the politicians have made little contribution to the development of educational policy since 1945 and parliament has, in consequence, been an accounting rather than a policy-making body.

Administration of education

Notwithstanding the elaborate provision for regional and local participation in education which has been a feature of all three major Education Acts—Part Two, 'Local Administration' is the longest part of the 1964 Education Act—the real control and direction of the New Zealand education system has, at least from 1914, been exercised by the central department, the only authority which controls more than one level of education. In addition to the central department with its head office in Wellington and three regional offices in Auckland, Wellington and Christchurch there are ten education boards, one in each of the legally defined education districts; school committees, one for each primary school; boards of governors, typically one for each secondary school; governing councils for the teachers' colleges and for the technical institutes; and, acting for the six universities, the University Grants Committee. Pre-school institutions, which are outside the statutory school system, have their own controlling authorities.

The Department of Education

Responsible for the department is the Minister of Education, who, in New Zealand, has always held cabinet rank. In 1970 the appointment of a parliamentary under-secretary marked either a greater political awareness of the importance and complexity of the Education portfolio, or possibly, reflected anxiety about the cost of education. In 1972 the incoming Labour administration did not appoint an under-secretary.

The Department of Education is structurally similar to other large government departments. Its administrative head is the director-general whose present title was changed from that of director by the 1964 Education Act. His immediate subordinates are two assistant directors-general, one dealing with professional and the other with administrative matters, and four directors, each in charge of a major division of the department: most of the senior officers are ex-teachers with a very real feeling for education.

The department's pre-eminence, its role of a triton among the minnows, is assured since it channels from funds appropriated by parliament for education the approved expenditure of its local partners. This leaves the other authorities—the University Grants Committee excepted—with little scope for initiative. Departmental primacy is further guaranteed by its authority to make regulations, by the influence of its senior officers on government educational policy-making, and by its control of the curricula of primary and secondary schools and teachers' colleges.

In recent years, the department has deliberately done much to involve local authorities and the teachers' organizations in the formulation of some major aspects of policy. Much of this has been concerned with curriculum development and with the reorganization of teacher training. The department's strategy of involvement and consultation has only limited application in the administrative sphere. However, the work of the two Standing Committees on Administration involves sustained consultation and planning. These committees, one for primary and the other for secondary education, bring together departmental officers and representatives from the national organizations of education boards and governing bodies, the Education Boards' Association and the Secondary School Boards' Association. The first Standing Committee, that for the primary sub-system, was set up in 1957 when relations between the boards and the department were particularly strained. The main task of the two committees is to help reconcile the interests of departmental and local authority administrators on matters of finance, accounting procedures, building programmes and school transport. In 1948, realizing that the point of tension was often too far removed from the point of action, the Department of Education established a regional office in Auckland 'to be the Head Office of the Education Department in Auckland' (Roberts, 1961, 18). Later, in 1960 and 1963, similar offices were opened in Christchurch and Wellington.

To these regional offices, whose structure deliberately mirrors that of the central department, is delegated much of the routine of educational administration formerly carried out by head office. District education boards, not always to their liking, and boards of governors are required to deal with their regional offices rather than, as before, directly with the department, though it has always been recognized that boards of governors have direct access, should they need it, to the minister. The senior regional officer, the superintendent, has both administrative and professional responsibilities, coordinates the work of branches in his office, provides educational leadership in his region, fosters good relations with the community at large, and when trouble threatens, tries to solve the problems, as a regional officer remarked, 'at the tadpole stage'.

Local administration

Thus there is a curious contradiction in the administration of education. On the one hand the existence of ten district education boards and a multiplicity of school committees and boards of governors seems to imply a considerable measure of local initiative and control; on the other hand, central financing and departmental control of curricula imply a large measure of direction and supervision from the centre. This dichotomy, inherent in the Education Act of 1877, had led by 1914 to the assumption of real authority by the department. Yet lay participation in educational administration has survived. In 1972, 25,000 laymen were working, sometimes at crosspurposes, in the interests of separate, largely isolated sectors of the education system, their energies more often devoted to the improvement of lavatories than to the advancement of learning.

Education boards

In the vanguard of this army are the members of the ten education boards, the second tier of the administrative structure of the primary school sub-system. The present statutory functions of the boards, which have between eight and sixteen members according to the size and population of the education district, are to 'establish, maintain, and control' state primary schools and certain secondary schools in their districts; to appoint teachers to their schools; to arrange for the

9

conveyance of children to and from school, and to pass on to school committees their annual government grant. In performing most of these duties, education boards are merely agents of the central department. Building programmes are subject to central approval; a departmental inspector is a member of every appointing committee and arrangements for the transport of pupils must be approved by the regional transport officer. Each board, however, independently of the Department of Education, appoints its own administrative staff of which the senior executive is the secretary-manager or general manager.

So greatly have the powers of the education boards been eroded since their hey-day around the turn of the century that the suggestion is made from time to time that they should be eliminated from the administrative structure. But education board members argue that they and their administrative staff, being accessible to school committee members and parents in a way Department of Education officials, even in regional offices, can never be, constitute an essential safeguard against central bureaucracy.

School committees

Each education district is divided into school districts and although it was not the intention of the Education Act of 1877, there is normally one primary school and one school committee for each school district. School committees consist of from five to nine lay members (depending on the school roll) elected every two years by householders of the district. These committees have never fulfilled their original role of counterbalancing the powers of the education boards. Today a committee is simply the 'guardian of the local school' (Commission on Education, 1962, 73). As 'guardians' school committee members are responsible to their education board for the upkeep of school premises and the payment of the caretaker. Necessary funds are received from the government through the education board. Since the 1964 Education Act took away the right of committees to suspend a teacher, only two significant functions remain: to take part in the election of the education board and, since 1962, to decide, in consultation with the principals, whether or not thirty minutes of religious instruction a week shall be allowed in their schools.

On the other hand, the committees' negative powers are considerable, for they are not tied by any code of ethics, formal or informal, such as those for teachers and other professionals in the education service. They can, for example, frustrate principals or stir up trouble by encouraging staff members to express to them views which are in opposition to those of the head.

Despite fine-sounding official descriptions of school committees as the 'cornerstone' of the public school system's administrative structure, the most worthwhile work done now by them is to organize 'working bees' to improve the school grounds, and to master mind fund-raising ventures, the profits from which are used for projects attracting the government's dollar for dollar subsidy. A good case could be made for merging school committees with the non-statutory home and school or parent–teacher associations which are active in most primary schools.

Although education board officials praise school committees (Mitchell, 1968, 41; Roberts, 1961, 61), they have never pressed the Department of Education to put a representative of the New Zealand School Committees' Federation, a national organization representing over 1,200 school committees, on the Standing Committee on Administration (Primary). Remits from the federation's annual conference to the department often, it is alleged, go unanswered for months, although the Minister of Education usually writes to each newly-elected president of the federation to assure him that his door is 'always open to representation from the Federation' (Ingle, 1967, 61).

Boards of governors

Except for a very few secondary schools which have chosen to associate themselves for administrative purposes with their district education boards, most New Zealand secondary schools are independently governed by their own boards. Before the establishment of the regional offices, all these had direct access to the Department of Education. It has been suggested that the regional offices in Christchurch and Wellington were forced on the department to protect itself from 'a multitude of school boards making incessant claims . . . for finance and amenities' (Mitchell, 1968, 36). Whatever the true circumstances of their origin, one of the principal functions of the regional offices now is to provide secondary school boards with administrative services similar to those provided by education boards for their school committees.

The reason for the administrative divorce at the local level between primary and secondary education is historical: the national school system created by the 1877 Education Act was essentially a primary one. 'We cannot afford,' one member of the House of Representatives said during a debate on the 1877 Education Bill, 'to provide for the higher branches of an educational system in this country; we must be content . . . with a measure of this kind, which will enable the State to secure, as far as possible, that there shall not be in the colony a child growing up in ignorance' (*NZPD*, 1877, vol. 25, 231). The 'higher branches' evolved separately and the precedent established in the nineteenth century that each secondary school should have its own board of governors subordinate only to the Department of Education has been generally followed ever since. But present day governing bodies are pale shadows of their nineteenth-century forbears, having lost a great deal of ground to the central department. Yet it is still true, as the Commission on Education stated, that the autonomy of boards of governors has 'never been curbed by central control to the same degree as that of the education boards' (Commission on Education, 1962, 79).

Broadly speaking, boards of governors fulfil the same functions for secondary schools as do education boards and school committees for primary schools. The general constitution of secondary school governing bodies is laid down in sections 50 and 51 of the 1964 Education Act. These state that a board shall consist of not fewer than nine and not more than eleven members, five elected by parents, one appointed by the education board of the district and the others representative of community groups which may include employers in local industries, the former pupils' association of the school, the school committees of contributing primary schools or the university which serves the area. Teachers are still unrepresented, a fact many resent when it is possible for a pupil to be elected by the parents. Although hedged about by departmental regulations and rulings, and restricted in their activities by the smallness of the annual government grant, boards still have enough independence to make membership of them both challenging and satisfying. Their most important right, and one which they jealously guard in the face of teacher-criticism, is that of appointing the principal with whom they share responsibility for the management of the school. 'It is generally assumed,' an unpublished Department of Education circular advised secondary school principals in 1961, 'that the board is supreme on administrative matters and on appointment of staff (although the principal must be consulted) and that the principal bears the main responsibility in matters of curriculum, syllabuses of instruction, allocation of duties among staff and the control of pupils.'

If three or more boards of governors in neighbouring localities wish to act in concert on matters of common interest they may apply to the Minister of Education for an Order in Council setting up a secondary schools' council. The council, on which each member school is equally represented, provides a central office for the secretarial and accounting work of the boards and, when necessary, facilitates the co-ordination of secondary education in its area.

Nationally, the Secondary School Boards' Association formed in 1945 keeps the needs and wishes of its members constantly before the department. Short of finance, and without research staff, the association has not been very successful in gaining concessions from the department. The fault, however, does not lie primarily with the association's executive; so long as individual secondary school boards—and individual education boards, too, for that matter—believe that the direct approach to the department is the most effective way to get things done, their national bodies can be little more than information agencies.

The government of tertiary institutions

The 1964 Education Act placed technical institutes and teachers' colleges under the 'control and direction' of the director-general, and although both have evolved since that date to a point where they can legitimately claim to be fully-fledged tertiary institutions, they have not yet been granted an appropriate degree of professional and administrative autonomy. The controlling authorities of technical institutes have little more than the limited powers of secondary school boards, while teachers' colleges were, until 1968, controlled by sub-committees of their district education boards. Since then teachers' college councils, widely representative of professional and academic interests, but with as yet undetermined authority, especially in curricular matters, have been established.

Principals of technical institutes and teachers' colleges must envy the autonomy guaranteed the universities by their Grants Committee of seven persons, government-appointed but independent of ministerial or departmental control, four not directly connected with the universities but with an intimate knowledge of their life and conventions, and three university teachers. Its brief, as stated in the Universities Act of 1961, is to inquire into the financial needs, the educational programmes and the development plans of the six universities. In the light of its assessments of the needs of the university system it is 'to advise and make recommendations to the Government of New Zealand through the Minister [of Education] on any matters relating to University education and research requiring the consideration of the Government'. The University Grants Committee in New Zealand, as in Great Britain, advises the government about the appropriate size of the total quinquennial grant and about the distribution of 'this grant between the different possible recipients once it is made available' (Committee on Higher Education, 1963, 235).

Among the sub-committees of the New Zealand University Grants Committee the one of most immediate concern to university teachers and students alike is the Curriculum Committee which comprises representatives of all the universities, the chairman of the Grants Committee, and the director-general of education. Its main task is to ensure equivalence between universities of courses for degrees and diplomas and an awareness by each university of the academic legislation of the others. In recent years the work of the Curriculum Committee has been stringently criticized. It has been described by students as a committee 'which meets rarely and conducts most of its business by circulated resolutions' (NZ University Students' Association, 1969, 3), and by senior university administrators as 'a quasi-legal body which wastes time and energy and paper on minor matters' (Conference of Universities, 1969, 15). Certainly, the committee rarely objects to proposed regulations.

For the most part, however, the machinery created by the Universities Act to administer and control higher education in New Zealand has worked satisfactorily although it is sometimes suggested that, as well as the University Grants Committee, there should also be a continuing body for university consultation representative of the separate university councils. There is no desire, however, to reintroduce the kind of central machinery that existed in the days of the federal University of New Zealand; the separate universities are too jealous of their independence.

Within each university, senior academics, together with elected representatives of the sub-professorial staff and of the student body, control the development and direction of academic policy-making through a senate or professorial or academic board, faculties or boards of studies, departments and numerous ad hoc committees. As in most Commonwealth universities, the formulation of administrative policy and the control of financial matters is entrusted to a council on which, besides academic, industrial, business and other interests are represented. As university affairs become more complex, the decisions of these predominantly lay councils are increasingly being influenced and guided by the advice of the vice-chancellors and their senior administrative officers.

Administrative evolution

Even though a much greater degree of decentralization has been advocated by Labour Party spokesmen on education, radical shifts in the balance of administrative power are unlikely to take place in the immediate future. Control from the centre, as at present, seems inevitable while the system is financed centrally. And there is no enthusiasm for a local education rate. Furthermore, the national teachers' organizations favour a centralized system because it ensures equitable schemes for appointments and promotions, for the supply of classroom equipment and for the provision of school facilities generally. Post-war, the Department of Education has been urged to delegate greater financial powers but it is unlikely that any New Zealand government will hand over large sums of money to local authorities for the free exercise of their educational ideas 'without clear accounting of how the money is to be spent or assurance of the minimum standards that it must demand on behalf of all the nation's children' (Commission on Education, 1962, 94).

New Zealand experience has shown that centralized control is not necessarily inconsistent with a substantial measure of local administration and the maintenance of community interest in education.

Officials believe that further decentralization, especially in the economically troubled times which may lie ahead now that Great Britain, New Zealand's main market for primary produce, has entered the European Economic Community, would make more difficult the attainment of the department's blameless twin objectives: economical administration on the one hand and sound educational progress on the other.

To secure these objectives a balance of power between centralism and localism should allow the administrative system to function without frustration or waste. Attempts to achieve this balance, first begun during the directorship of N. T. Lambourne (1933-40), were intensified after 1945. Since 1962, when the Commission on Education recommended the fostering of greater 'local activity', the Department of Education has increased its efforts to consult groups outside the department and to involve them in the formulation of policy. The result has been a marked improvement in the administrative atmosphere; consultation has produced among local educational authorities and interest groups a better understanding and appreciation of the political and economic factors which often affect departmental decision-making. It may well be, as a former Chief Inspector of Primary Schools has suggested, 'that in the New Zealand context consultation, negotiation and joint-planning constitute a preferable alternative to decentralization' (Ewing, 1970, 8).

2

The legal basis, finance and official policy

Educational legislation is rarely the subject of intense political debate although the first national Education Act—'an Act to make provision for the Further Education of the People of New Zealand' —was passed by the General Assembly in 1877 only after prolonged, vigorous and often passionate argument. This Act, originally concerned almost entirely with creating a national network of efficient free secular primary schools, remains the foundation of the present complex and extensive educational structure. It finally decided the question of compulsion, the relationship of church and state in education and the pattern of administration and finance.

The 1914 Education Act was largely a consolidating measure made necessary by developments in secondary education and administration. Forty-three amendments to this Act were made in the fifty years which elapsed before, in the absence of a written constitution, the Education Act of 1964 became the legal basis of the education system. It brought the terminology of the law up-to-date, transferred to statute law certain important matters dealt with by regulations, incorporated amending legislation and deleted some of the provisions of the 1914 Education Act.

Neither Act, however, departed from the principles established in 1877 as the Ministers of Education in 1914 and 1964, J. Allen and A. E. Kinsella respectively, stressed. Kinsella especially emphasized the routine, even utilitarian nature of the pending legislation by saying his Bill was not an attempt to provide a blueprint for the future. He refused to enact into law the recommendations made by a Commission on Education in 1962 on improvements in salaries, ancillary staffing, curriculum development, the training of teachers and the reduction of class sizes. The Act was intended to lay down broad outlines only, he argued, and to preserve its flexibility most of the commission's suggestions would be better dealt with through regulations than through embodiment in legislation.

The Education Act of 1964

In its general format the 1964 Education Act followed that of the English Education Act of 1944 but similarity ended there. The English statute brought about quite fundamental changes in the nation's education system; the New Zealand Act introduced little that was new and nothing that was revolutionary.

The first two parts of the Act deal with administration. The first, 'Central Administration', sets out the powers of the Minister of Education and his senior civil servant, the director-general of education, over the Department of Education. The second part of the Act, 'Local Administration', deals with the functions of the district education boards, school committees and boards of governors.

The third part, 'Establishment of Schools', describes the kinds of educational institutions under the administrative surveillance of the department and lays down who can attend them. Through its power to make regulations the department controls the curricula of primary and secondary schools and the teachers' colleges. Clause 85 highlights the non-selective character of the secondary schools. 'Every secondary school and every secondary department shall . . . give free secondary education to pupils who have completed a year's work in form two or who have attained the age of fourteen years.' The conditions under which religious instruction can be given in state schools are also detailed.

The fourth part of the Act, 'Enrolment and Attendance of Pupils', requires in section 109 that every child shall be enrolled at a state or registered private school 'from the time when he attains the age of six years until he attains the age of fifteen years'. A child more than two miles from school or transport is exempted until the age of seven.

Other sections of part four outline further conditions under which exemption certificates may be granted and deal with the compulsory enrolment of school-age children who are 'suffering from disability of body or mind of such magnitude as to require special education'. The Act warns against the employment of children under the age of fifteen during school hours. Education authorities are required, if necessary, to appoint Attendance Officers (the Truant Officers of earlier legislation) empowered during school hours 'on production of a distinctive badge' to 'detain any child who appears . . . to be of school age and is not then present in school and to question him as to his age, name and address, the school at which he is enrolled, and the reason of his absence from school'. His parent or guardian may then be summoned and is liable to a fine not exceeding $40. The powers of principals, school committees and boards of governors to suspend or expel children 'for gross misconduct or incorrigible disobedience' are specified in a further section but the emphasis is put on getting such children back to school quickly whenever possible.

The fifth and sixth parts of the Act refer to teachers, their registration, appointment, conditions of employment and rights of appeal. Earlier legislation constituting a Central Advisory Committee to supervise the primary appointments system, legislation which reflected the bitterness and friction created by appointment procedures in the still-remembered past, was incorporated in the principal Act. However, the 1964 Act's requirement that each of the ten education boards maintain its own Primary Teachers' Appointment Appeal Board was waived in an Education Amendment Act in 1968. There is now one national Appeal Board.

Part seven, 'Inspection of Schools', is brief. All private schools must, as before, be registered with the central department and be open to inspection as with state primary and secondary schools and technical institutes.

And finally, part eight, 'General Provisions' tries to allow for unforeseen contingencies which could not conveniently be covered elsewhere in the Act. A potentially interesting provision of this kind is that which permits trustees of private schools to place them under the control of district education boards.

In spite of its consolidating function the Bill did contain some provisions that were new or nearly new. In section 70, for the first time in New Zealand educational legislation, financial assistance was provided for pre-school institutions. Improvements in rural secondary education were anticipated by section 86 which empowered the Minister of Education to establish 'composite schools' in larger rural centres. The minister explained that, although in general it was intended that these would be Form I–VI schools, the 'widely-written' term, 'composite schools', was used so as not to preclude experimentation in other forms of combined primary–secondary schooling.

Sections 89 and 90 incorporated a brief but extremely important amendment Act of 1963 which had recognized technical institutes as tertiary, rather than secondary institutions, though still working under what are basically secondary regulations—a great source of vexation.

Finally, unremarked upon but surely not unnoticed by members of parliament was the significance of Section 192 in Part Eight. It stated, 'The Governor-General may from time to time, by Order in Council, make regulations providing for the making of grants, out of money appropriated for the purpose, to the governing bodies of registered private schools.' This unprecedented authority to assist private schools should have evoked a strong reaction from those members of parliament who claimed to be the watchdogs of the state system. That it did not, indicated how deeply compromised both the main political parties had already become on the highly-controversial issue of state aid to private schools.

In fact, the only real controversy in an otherwise drab and tedious series of debates on a largely agreed measure was aroused by sections 157–61 of the Act, the so-called 'disciplinary sections', which made teachers liable to the same penalties for misdemeanours as the rest of the Public Service. The objections of the two national teachers' organizations, the New Zealand Educational Institute and the Post-Primary Teachers' Association, were echoed in debates by their parliamentary champions who claimed the provisions were unnecessary, unworkable and unprofessional. Even in a modified form, the teachers continued to oppose these sections of the law and the Post-Primary Teachers' Association in particular persisted in urging amendment. It was rewarded in 1969 when, after protracted negotiation, the Association gained through the Secondary and Technical Institute Teachers' Disciplinary Regulations what its General Secretary, (since 1973 Director of Secondary Education), called 'a new deal' (Boag, 1970, 14).

Since 1964, regulations and a number of amendment acts have extended, enlarged or varied the Act's provisions, but there have been no major basic changes in the original legislation. Coherent, comprehensive and flexible, the 1964 Education Act has fulfilled the purpose intended for it, that of providing the desired baseline for continuing educational change and development.

The Universities Act of 1961

By 1961 the law relating to higher education was also outmoded. Established in 1874 as a federal examining and degree-granting body on the lines of the University of London, the University of New Zealand during the post-war period of rapid growth in higher education, hindered more than helped its constituent colleges, which during the 1950s became fully responsible for all examining as well as teaching though their degrees continued to be awarded by the University of New Zealand. As the four constituent colleges moved further and further away from each other in research fields, teaching interests and curricula, they became increasingly restive at the restraints imposed by membership of a federal organization. By 1958 each of the constituent colleges had become a university in name, but they still remained under the umbrella of the University of New Zealand.

In 1959 a three-man committee was appointed by the government to inquire into the universities and, in its comprehensive list of recommendations, gave priority to the need for administrative re-organization. It urged that each constituent university 'be granted the status, privileges, powers, duties and responsibilities enjoyed by a free and separate university', subject only to the over-sight of a University Grants Committee.

The government acted quickly. The Universities Act of 1961, 'An Act to Make Better Provision for the Advancement of University Education in New Zealand', dissolved the University of New Zealand and transferred some of its functions, including its degree-granting powers, to the individual universities, each of which was formally constituted by its own Act 'for the advancement of knowledge and the dissemination and maintenance thereof by teaching and research' during the 1961 session of parliament. To fill the gap left by the federal university, the first part of the Universities Act provided for a University Grants Committee (the chairman of which is appointed by the governor general after consultation between the Minister of Education and the vice chancellors of the New Zealand universities). The second part created a Universities Entrance Board which is responsible for university entrance standards and directly influences the work of the secondary schools by laying down the syllabuses for the university examinations it controls—Entrance, Bursaries, Scholarship and Fine Arts Preliminary.

The third part of the Act provided for a Vice-Chancellors' Committee to 'consider any matter relating to the Universities and [to] report or make recommendations thereon to the University Grants Committee and also, if it thinks fit, to any university'. Its duties were similar to those previously carried out by the vice-chancellor and senate of the University of New Zealand. Since 1961, within this legal framework, the New Zealand university system has expanded rapidly.

Legislation relating to technical and vocational education

While the 1964 Education Act and the 1961 Universities Act constitute the main legal basis of the New Zealand education system, technical and trades training are the subject of separate legislation.

Following recommendations made by the Commission on Apprenticeship, an Apprentices Act was passed in 1948. This provided for the appointment of a Commissioner of Apprenticeship to improve and supervise the training and education of apprentices throughout New Zealand, and to foster collaboration between the Department of Education and the schools on the one hand, and the Department of Labour and the trades on the other. In the same year a Trades Certification Act authorized the establishment of a Trades Certification Board chaired by a nominee of the Minister of Education to develop examinations for apprentices. As each new trade examination was established, the Department of Education ceased to accept candidates for the appropriate examination of the City and Guilds of London Institute for which it had acted as agent since 1894.

The Trades Certification Act of 1948 was concerned only with training and examining tradesmen; not until ten years later, when the place of technicians in industry had become more clearly recognized, was similar legislation for their training, the Technicians Certification Act, passed. Almost a decade later the Minister of Labour, following certain recommendations of the Commission of Inquiry into Vocational Training and urged on by both sides of the building industry, introduced what he called 'skeleton legislation'. It established technician training councils to promote and administer training schemes. It was intended to remove certain difficulties which had previously prevented the full development of co-ordinated industrial and educational courses. Legally it recognized and protected the technician cadet. And it allowed, following the model of the British Industrial Training Act of 1964, the imposition of levies on employers engaged in an industry to help meet the cost of appropriate technician training schemes.

This Technicians Training Act of 1967 was, for New Zealand, a pioneering measure. It was followed in 1968 by the Vocational Training Council Act which authorized the creation of a council, widely representative of industry and education, to oversee the planning, co-ordination and development of all vocational training courses. The Vocational Training Council replaced an earlier Council for Technical Education which, being purely advisory to the Minister of Education and having no full-time staff, had failed to function satisfactorily.

The Technicians Training Act and the Vocational Training Council Act have created a legal framework around which an efficient and up-to-date system of technical and vocational education and training may be built. It is too early yet to say how completely the new legislation will meet the present and future needs of industry and commerce.

Adult or continuing education

Historically, adult and informal education started with the founding of Mechanics' Institutes, Scientific and Mutual Improvement Societies and Athenaeums in the nineteenth century and, after 1915, with the support given to the Workers' Educational Association. In New Zealand as in Great Britain the Workers' Educational Association was the 'school' of many Labour movement leaders before the accession to power of a Labour Government in 1935. The impact of the Workers' Educational Association outside the four main centres was initially limited, but a grant from the Carnegie Foundation in 1937 and in 1938 an amendment to the Education Act by a sympathetic government, which created a Council of Adult Education and made funds available to the university colleges, made it possible for the Workers' Educational Association to extend its adult education activities and services. These funds were substantially increased by the Adult Education Act of 1947, 'an Act to Promote and Foster Adult Education and the Cultivation of the Arts'. A National Council and four Regional Councils were established, each under the aegis of a constituent college of the university. When the University of New Zealand was dissolved in 1961 new legislation was needed which was passed in the Act of 1963. This made a re-structured National Council adviser to the Director of Education and the University Grants Committee on matters relating to adult education, abolished the Regional Councils, and authorized each university to develop its own Department of University Extension. These departments offer the general public and, in particular the professions, an increasing number of courses.

The remarkable rise in the demand for what the Americans call continuing education has only been partially met, since 1945, by the formal adult education agencies. Their work has been supplemented, either directly or indirectly, by a bewildering number of non-statutory organizations, notably the Workers' Educational Association and the Countrywomen's Co-ordinating Committee. But more significantly, the greater proportion of further education students are enrolled in evening vocational classes at technical institutes or hobby classes offered by many secondary schools. Indeed, the rapid growth of what the 1964 Education Act refers to as 'technical and continuation classes' put such financial pressure on the Department of Education in the late 1960s that it was forced for a time to restrict the number of hobby classes which schools could offer. As the fees paid by further education students are retained by the controlling authorities of the secondary schools, this restriction sharply reduced the incomes of some already impecunious governing bodies.

Education finance

Compared with that of the USA or Canada or England, the finance of education in New Zealand is relatively simple, for it is collected and largely disbursed centrally. The public and private sectors are financed separately. Section 9 (1) of the 1964 Education Act states the position succinctly:

> All amounts payable for the expenses of the Department [of Education], and all amounts payable under this Act to

Education Boards and other controlling authorities for educational and other prescribed purposes . . . shall be paid out of money from time to time appropriated by Parliament for the purposes of this Act.

Money appropriated by parliament is the sole substantial source of educational revenue. There is no specific education tax, no provision for the raising of education loans, and no local taxes for education. Sometimes it is suggested that a grave mistake was made in 1877 by deleting a clause of the Education Bill which, in order to remind parents of their responsibilities, proposed that one-eighth of the cost of education should be met by a system of local rating. But there is no likelihood that in the foreseeable future any New Zealand government will attempt to depart from the almost century-long practice of centralized financing. The Commission on Education which reported in 1962 was strongly in favour of its retention. In particular it stressed the disparities in educational provision likely to occur from the introduction of local rating which would not be wholly eliminated by rate-deficiency grants. The commission's view reflected what most New Zealanders felt, namely that local rating would reduce the ability of the school system to offer all children truly equal educational opportunity, because inevitably some school authorities would then have more money to spend than others.

In fact inequalities already exist from district to district and from school to school as a result of a 'subsidy scheme' which allows locally-raised funds to attract matching government subsidies to purchase specified facilities, for example swimming baths, assembly halls and gymnasiums. Subsidizing voluntary contributions began in 1900 (although the present scheme dates only from 1948) and has become accepted policy, especially for primary schools. In the secondary schools most of what is provided under subsidy in the primary schools is obtainable by direct grant, although the special subsidy provisions for swimming baths and gymnasiums still apply. Government subsidies are attractive and as a result school authorities and parent–teacher associations are cast more often than they might wish as organizers of school fairs, galas, raffles and similar money-raising activities. Yet in spite of all this, the total amount provided directly by parents and other donors for school equipment and amenities, including the small annual sports and library fee parents of secondary school pupils are asked to pay, comes to only a little over 1 per cent of the annual education vote.

University finance

The universities, like the rest of the education system, depend upon a parliamentary appropriation from central tax funds for the greater part of their finance. Since 1963, it has included funds for adult education, and is subject to Cabinet approval. After this has been given, the money is paid by Treasury to the Department of Education, which then pays over an allocated sum to each university, so the department is simply a distributing agent.

In addition to Treasury grants, some university income comes from tuition fees, but much of this is taxpayers' money because the government provides an extensive range of awards, grants and bursaries. Other funds come from benefactions and endowments, but when the latter are from lands vested in the universities in their early years (the South Island Universities of Otago and Canterbury are especially well-endowed), an equal amount is subtracted from their annual grants. (This practice is also adopted by the Department of Education to ensure financial equality among state secondary schools, the older of which, when established by private Acts of Parliament in the nineteenth century, were endowed with extensive land holdings.)

Control of spending

Control of educational spending is exercised in a number of ways by parliament or its servants. The most influential of these servants —there are some who would substitute 'master' for 'servant'—is undoubtedly Treasury. Through its control of the national purse-strings, Treasury and the Minister of Finance exert considerable influence on the Department of Education's planning. Because Treasury's prime function appears to be to save money by limiting educational expenditure to that which is unavoidable, many critics of its influence complain that economic expediency too often out-weighs educational desirability. They contend, further, that the positive management of resources within a framework of long-term educational goals is thus neglected or made impossible.

Responsibility for checking the legality of departmental expenditure lies within the province of officials of the Audit Office, who annually inspect the documents and records, not only of state departments, but also of universities, local bodies and many public corporations. Each year the controller and auditor-general reports directly to parliament. His report is concerned mainly with the 'correctness' of expenditure and although it may be critical, the Audit Office does not concern itself with policy to the same extent as the Treasury.

The wide powers enjoyed by Treasury and the Audit Office do not mean that parliament has abdicated its responsibilities to senior public servants. Members are particularly jealous of their right to oversee the work, and especially the spending, of government departments. The opposition is constantly on the alert to detect injustices, inadequacies or anomalies arising from the actions of the government or its servants. No Minister of the Crown can afford to treat lightly private members' questions, careless answers to which, Ministers of Education have discovered, can lead to embarrassing situations.

Parliament's most effective form of supervision lies in its far-reaching authority to investigate departmental spending. Until 1962, the permanent head of every department, usually accompanied by his senior finance officers, appeared each year before the Public Accounts Committee, a bi-partisan committee of the House of Representatives (New Zealand has a unicameral system of parliamentary government) to justify his department's estimates for the next twelve months.

In 1962 the work of the Public Accounts Committee was taken over by the Public Expenditure Committee. Set up each session by the House, this committee examines the public accounts and the accounts of such corporations, undertakings and organizations as are in receipt of money from parliament, 'in such manner and to such extent as the Committee sees fit'.

This non-expert committee does not merely ask how a department intends to spend money voted it by parliament, but later checks on the way it has been spent. Each year, during the parliamentary recess, sub-committees of the Public Expenditure Committee travel throughout New Zealand investigating the work of one or more departments. So that the committee can see a department in its 'normal working dress' only brief notice of an intended visit is given the minister in charge or his senior officers.

The newly-created committee investigated educational expenditure first because, according to its spokesman, R. D. Muldoon, the Education Vote had increased more rapidly each year than any other to a point where the Department of Education had become one of the largest spending departments of state.

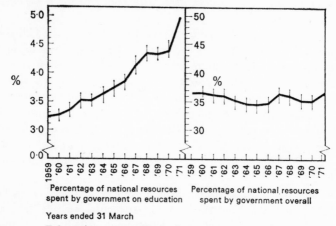

Percentage of national resources spent by government on education   Percentage of national resources spent by government overall

Years ended 31 March

Figure 1   Education expenditure increases, 1959–71 (Source: Treasury Graph, March 1971)

The inquiry occupied two years; the committee's final report showed clearly that it was not prepared to treat any educational shibboleths as sacred. It condemned, on financial grounds, the department's decision to set up separate training institutions for secondary teachers, said that the Commission on Education had been wrong in 1962 to recommend that teachers' colleges be restricted in size to 750 students, and suggested ways of mitigating the disadvantages of large enrolments. It accused the Department of Education of using money intended for its Child Welfare Division for other purposes; it complimented some education boards and criticized others on their standards of building maintenance; it commented on the efficiency of local educational administration which it judged to range from very high to, in the case of one large education board, 'a state of semi-confusion'.

The Public Expenditure Committee, however, can only check and recommend; it cannot compel a department to take, or desist from taking, a particular line of action. Although both the Department of Education and the local controlling authorities have acted on a number of the committee's suggestions, the department has declined to act on criticisms of practices which it believes to be outside the competence of laymen to judge. To the committee's complaint that the maintenance of separate primary and secondary teachers' colleges was wasteful, the department replied sharply that 'The Education Department advises that the Committee's recommendation involves a number of complex issues and a great deal more study is necessary before Government could be committed to a change of policy' (Public Expenditure Committee, 1966, 8).

Investment in education

When selecting the Department of Education as the target for their first inquiry, the Public Expenditure Committee pointed out that the cost of education was rising more sharply than that of any other single service. The trend has continued. In 1950–1 education costs represented 7·5 per cent of total government expenditure; in 1960–1 the percentage had risen to 9·45 and in 1971–2 it was 16·4 per cent.

Marked as they are, these increases do not mean that public education in New Zealand is now lavishly funded. They are, in part, a result of growing enrolments, falling money values and increasing aid to the private sector. The proportion of the gross national product devoted to education, a more accurate measure of a nation's investment in education, has not risen substantially in the last decade. 'Spending on education in New Zealand,' an economist told the Commission on Education in 1961, 'is considerably lower in relation to our gross national product than spending in the United States and somewhat less than in the United Kingdom, and the difference between us and the United Kingdom becomes more obvious when one takes account of the relatively high proportion of our population which is of school and university age' (Commission on Education, 1962, 141). In 1964 education's share of the gross national product in Britain was 5·3 per cent; in New Zealand in 1967 it was 4·2 per cent. A National Development Conference which reported in 1969 recommended that if, as should be the case, New Zealand governments are to look upon their outlay on education as an investment, somewhat analogous to expenditure on physical assets, which will yield a return in terms of increased efficiency and economic growth, then the proportion of the gross national product allocated to education should be substantially increased. A target of 5·2 per cent, to be reached by 1972–3, was suggested. In 1970–1 the proportion of the gross national product actually allocated to education was 4·9 per cent, 3 per cent greater than it had been in 1945–6 (*A to J*, 1970, E–1, 9).

Official policy making: the Minister and Department

Within the legal framework and subject to the checks imposed on it by the Public Expenditure Committee, the Department of Education is responsible for the formulation of a great deal of educational policy. Indeed the fear is sometimes expressed that anonymous public servants and not politicians accountable to electors, have taken charge of the educational system. This is denied from time to time. A. E. Kinsella, Minister of Education from 1963 to 1969, for example, said that officers of his department operated in accordance with government policy and that it was nonsense to suggest that they made policy themselves (*Evening Post*, 15 October 1969). Nevertheless since 1945 the fear has been kept alive by the inactivity of post-war governments in the field of education. In these circumstances it is virtually impossible to distinguish sharply between policy-making and administrative decision-making. The position was well summarized by C. E. Beeby (Director of Education from 1940 to 1960) when he commented (1956, 8): 'Policy not only determines ways and means but is in some measure itself determined by the ways and means chosen to put it into operation. . . . Some major adjustments will inevitably result from administrative decisions made within the rather sketchy framework of stated policy.'

As mentioned earlier, party politics plays little part in the formulation of educational policy in New Zealand and post-war legislation has, for the most part, reiterated long-established principles of policy. Consequently Ministers of Education have relied heavily on their senior departmental administrators. Rarely are politics initiated by a minister, even by newly appointed ministers who were sharp critics of existing practices while in opposition. A minister's freedom to innovate is curtailed by the situation he inherits and by constraints on spending. However, major ultimate decisions remain with the government so that the Minister of Education always has the last word. He can, for example, decide—possibly to the discomfiture of his senior officers—where his active interest lies. He has, in short, the authority to veto, to sanction or promote policies for himself. When alternative lines of action are suggested to the government he has to choose between them—a choice often coloured by an appreciation of political rather than educational consequences. Finally, as education's champion in the Cabinet, the minister negotiates for the funds his department needs.

His effectiveness depends largely upon his vigour and enthusiasm —and an adequate departmental briefing. Because he has to relate his decision-making to that of the prime minister, the cabinet, the treasury and others at the apex of the government machine, his standing in the ministerial hierarchy is all-important in a centrally financed system. Upon it may depend his ability to secure the additional 0·5 per cent of gross national product which will allow for some experimentation and flexibility.

The prestige of the Minister of Education varies from government to government, but post-war education has not been a popular portfolio, partly because, since 1949, it has seldom been a stepping stone to more senior cabinet rank, and partly because aspirants to ministerial status have realized the thanklessness of fighting education's battles during a period of unprecedented growth, and consequently of unprecedented expenditure, in the system. They know that there is always an element of the 'anti-government' about a Department of Education which a former British Secretary of State for Education said, 'must fight for resources at times that other people find inconvenient' (Boyle, Crosland and Kogan, 1971, 143). Spending ministries are rarely popular with ambitious politicians.

On the other hand their interlocking functions make good relations between minister and department essential. In particular the political head, generally an amateur administrator, must have confidence in the permanent head, the director-general, who is a professional. On him the minister must lean heavily for advice, and the nature of his recommendations and advice will depend upon whether the director-general sees his role as that of innovator or manager. Most, but not all (George Hogben, in charge of the department for nearly sixteen

31

years, and C. E. Beeby, were outstanding exceptions), see themselves as executives first and innovators second.

This is not surprising because—Hogben and Beeby were again notable exceptions—this very senior public servant is usually chosen on the basis of seniority within the Department of Education. It has been suggested that a future government determined on educational change may well be advised, when selecting a permanent head, to look beyond those with a vested interest in the status quo. Probably such a break with tradition would be disliked by the teachers' professional bodies on the ground that a newcomer would not understand the problems of the education service.

Whatever the justification for this belief the 1964 Education Act reduced it by creating an elaborate superstructure in the department, which freed the director-general from much of his former direct responsibility for the day-to-day running of the national system. His key functions now (besides general oversight of his department) are to provide the minister with necessary professional information, to advise him and then to ensure that the department puts into operation government policy which is in fact mostly its own. It is unusual for a minister not to accept the advice given him by his experts—although he may do so with reservations. Only for urgent financial or political reasons would most ministers ignore departmental recommendations and pursue an independent policy.

Senior officials of the department, therefore, play a significant part in the formulation of policy. From time to time, some of them antagonize the teachers by their apparent self-conviction that they alone have all the experience and inside knowledge necessary to make correct decisions. It was these men—no women have ever occupied top administrative positions in the New Zealand Department of Education although they have done so with success in England—to whom the Labour Party spokesman on education referred in 1969 when he urged the government to 'hobble' senior officers because 'they held too much unrestrained power' (*Evening Post*, 15 October 1969).

Such criticism is comparatively rare. The departmental administrators are usually left alone to develop educational policy. Their autonomy derives from two sources: first, general public satisfaction with the public school system—frequent letters to the editor notwithstanding—and second, the slowness of both major political parties to evolve their own sets of long-range educational goals. Only the department has been able to provide continuity and consistency in policy-making.

This consistency does not imply that an official philosophy of education underlies all departmental decisions. The department, its director, A. E. Campbell, told the Commission on Education in New Zealand, has no 'philosophy of education', if that means an organized body of thought in which educational ideas, values and practices are related to fundamental beliefs about the nature of man, his place in the universe and the final meaning of life, but it does have a fairly definite set of liberal objectives designed to ensure the maintenance of certain minimum requirements and the encouragement of progressive developments (Campbell, 1960, 22–4).

Influence of commissions and consultative committees

Far-reaching changes in education are seldom initiated by the government, or even by a department–government coalition. Before a government will sanction a major change—for innovation inevitably costs money—it must be convinced there is a real demand for it. To give a particular problem full consideration and to afford interested organizations the opportunity to air their views, the minister may decide to follow the well-established British tradition and set up an ad hoc committee of inquiry with precise terms of reference, an independent chairman and members chosen for their experience and impartiality. Such advisory committees may deal with one problem and then cease to exist (for example, the Consultative Committee on Teacher Training), or they may have a continuous existence (for example, the National Advisory Council on Teacher Training).

In the immediate post-war period extensive use was made of ad hoc committees, variously titled. More recently ephemeral advisory committees seem to be less popular and have been replaced by relatively permanent committees set up by statute or by cabinet or ministerial directive. Between 1960 and 1972 the National Government did not use educational committees of inquiry as extensively as its Labour predecessor. There was, in fact, less need, because of the widespread inquiries into the state of education carried out during Labour's term of office from 1957 to 1960.

In 1959, in partial fulfilment of an election promise, the Minister of Education, P. O. Skoglund, appointed a Committee on the New Zealand Universities under the chairmanship of Sir David Hughes Parry, Emeritus Professor of English Law, University of London, to advise the government on the reform of the federal University of New Zealand. As soon as this committee had reported (which it did after three months, at the end of 1959), the minister set up, on 15 February 1960, a Commission on Education with a wide mandate to investigate the state school system. In a letter to the chairman, Sir George Currie, Vice-Chancellor of the University of New Zealand, the minister asked that he and his ten commissioners conduct:

> a full and impartial enquiry into the publicly controlled school system of this country, neither unduly hurried nor unduly prolonged, with opportunity for the Commission to take and sift a wide range of evidence, to initiate and carry through investigation of its own that it judges to be necessary, and, finally, to bring down a report which will enable us to see more clearly the direction of educational development and which will recommend specific lines of action.

The commission served, as intended, as a forum for public opinion beyond parliament or press; it gave both minister and Department of Education access to the views of experts and specialists outside the school system. It forced the country, as the introduction to the commission's 850-page report says, 'to take stock of its educational situation' (Commission on Education, 1962, 3). Asked both to evaluate the work of the existing system and to recommend guidelines for its future development, the members of the Currie Commission approached their task cautiously and with what some critics felt was a lack of reforming zeal. As a result, the unanimous report of the commission presented to the Minister of Education in June 1962, recommended fewer fundamental changes in the public school system than many hoped it would.

Nevertheless the Currie Commission bears the stamp of a worthwhile committee of inquiry. It produced a report that helped all interested parties appreciate more fully the issues at stake (and there had been considerable confusion on this score in the preceding decade). It provided sound and practical advice for teachers, laymen and educational administrators alike, and it helped to create a climate of opinion favourable to the adoption of many of its recommendations. Although it is part of the folklore of New Zealand education that the only useful purpose served by such commissions (or whatever verbal variation is used to describe a committee of inquiry), is to provide reports for the mythical pigeonholes of the Department of Education, history in fact shows that such a general statement is 'mischievously untrue' (Renwick, 1970, 3). In the post-war period there is unquestionably a close correspondence between what education commissions, parliamentary committees, consultative committees, working parties, and, in matters of curriculum, syllabus revision committees, have recommended and what later has become government and departmental policy. The Currie report was no exception to this general rule although its influence on the Education Act of 1964 is not especially marked, the government preferring to implement many of the commission's recommendations through regulations, a common practice, of dubious propriety, in New Zealand.

3

Education interest groups

Since the total cost of education is met from national taxation and departmental regulations are binding on the whole system, the central authority is in an extremely strong position in New Zealand. But the architects of the school system did not intend the central bureaucracy to be all-powerful. Charles Bowen, sponsor of the 1877 Education Bill, described it as the most decentralizing Bill ever passed in any 'English country', in providing entirely for local administration, 'subject to ultimate central control in certain particulars, especially in matters of expenditure' (*NZPD*, 1877, vol. 24, 32). He assured the House that the expenditure on a central department and central staff would not be great. A fellow member of the House of Representatives, H. H. Lusk, was not convinced. He agreed that the Bill certainly did not propose to centralize everything in Wellington. 'But,' he insisted, 'it contains in itself the germs of such a proposal as would inevitably lead to that result' (*NZPD*, 1877, vol. 25, 188).

Time has proved Lusk right. Education boards, school committees and the once proudly autonomous governing bodies of secondary schools have now all been firmly brought to heel under the central department. Although the administrative framework erected by the 1877 Act has been preserved, the functions and powers of the central and local authorities have altered dramatically. School committees, to be sure, never occupied the important place which the legislators of 1877 intended, largely because, from the outset, most education boards pursued a calculated policy of district centralization by making each committee responsible for only one school and by hedging them about with regulations. The committees contributed to their own downfall by failing to exercise their statutory powers, in particular of compelling attendance. Within a few years effective control of public primary education passed to the education boards, which continued to exercise it almost unchecked by the central department—although not uncriticized—until near the turn of the century. Then gradually the Department of Education, with the whole-hearted support of the primary teachers' professional body, the New Zealand Educational Institute, began to undermine the independence of the boards, a process virtually completed by the centralization of the inspectorate in 1914. (Previously inspectors had been board officers and as such were frequently outspoken in their criticisms of departmental proposals.) In 1927–8 the department sought the complete abolition of the boards, only to be frustrated by their ability to rally political and popular support by appealing to provincial loyalties and a general suspicion of the faceless bureaucrats in Wellington. It is not that parents feel any conviction that greater local control is desirable or necessary. They are not unduly alarmed when educational experts from overseas criticize New Zealand's administrative arrangements as likely to destroy the spirit of adaptation to local environments and to promote an unenterprising conformity (Kandel, 1938). Such strictures are unknown, ignored, suffered in silence or resented; present arrangements work. That is all the pragmatic New Zealander asks. There is no enthusiasm for competing local systems of education, especially if this implies educational rating.

Local authorities

Although severely circumscribed financially and administratively, the local controlling bodies are not afraid to criticize and comment on departmental action or inaction and are not unheeded. A former Director of Education has remarked that, in his experience, when educational expenditure was being examined by treasury and cabinet with a view to effecting economies, the items least likely to be cut back were those in which the boards were vitally interested, while the most vulnerable items were those which could rely on no firm support outside the department.

While the local authorities prevent the formal organization from becoming monolithic, their checking power would be still greater if they acted in concert. Individual education boards and boards of governors frequently approach the department on their own account rather than through their national bodies, the New Zealand Education Boards' Association and the Secondary School Boards' Association. Members believe, with some justification, that more can often

37

be gained this way. In many cases, only when they have been re-buffed, do the boards seek the assistance of their associations.

As a pressure group the Education Boards' Association is more effective than the Secondary School Boards' Association. The former was given statutory recognition by the Education Act of 1964 and it has over the years been better led and better financed than its secondary counterpart whose effectiveness will always be limited as long as individual boards continue to appeal directly to the department. A permanent alliance, on the other hand, between the two associations would produce a very strong pressure group whose demands the department would find it difficult to ignore or shrug off. How effective even a temporary alliance could be was shown when, by clinging tenaciously to their little local powers, education boards and governing bodies frustrated suspected departmental in-tentions to reorganize the administrative structure along lines sugges-ted by the 1962 Commission, so preventing the elimination of what uninvolved expert opinion has, for many years, seen as the major weakness of the New Zealand education system, the gulf between the primary and secondary levels.

It is not surprising that other examples of joint action are hard to find. Within its own sphere of influence, the primary sub-system, the Education Boards' Association makes little effort to co-operate with the New Zealand School Committees' Federation, an interest group which tries valiantly but vainly to maintain pressure on the department. The Secondary School Boards' Association, for its part, consistently declines to make common cause with the secondary school teachers' national body, the Post-Primary Teachers' Associa-tion (Ingle, 1967).

Teachers' organizations

At the heart of the school system are the teachers' organizations, the New Zealand Educational Institute, usually referred to as 'the Institute', and the Post-Primary Teachers' Association. These or-ganizations, which both constrain and stimulate, try always to influence the department by applying the greatest amount of pressure in the most telling places. Neither, however, has the repu-tation for consistently tough negotiation won by the National Union of Teachers in England, and because one organization represents primary teachers and the other secondary teachers the department may not always, especially during salary negotiations, resist the temptation to play one organization off against the other.

Rather belatedly, at the eighty-sixth annual conference of the Institute in 1969 its president spoke of the need for a teachers' federation which would follow a common course in matters of common concern to teachers, whether primary or secondary, but would still leave freedom to each to continue vigorous activity in its own sphere of interest. Unity, not union, was the ideal, he said. His call was probably not unassociated with the emergence in the late 1960s of a third teachers' organization, the short-lived New Zealand National Union of Teachers, representing all levels of the teaching profession. It is doubtful, however, if any third organization will win much support: the Institute in particular, and the Post-Primary Teachers' Association to an increasing extent, are closely knit organizations with loyal memberships.

The Institute is probably the best organized and certainly the most successful multi-purpose pressure group within the education system. It has a large membership (almost all primary teachers and primary teachers' college lecturers in the country belong), it is financially in a very sound condition and seldom has leadership crises. The Institute's executive is in constant touch with all the branches and consults them when pressing a case with the Department. The close and cordial liaison between their administrative heads ensures good Institute-department relations which go back a long way to the era before 1914 when the Institute and the fledgling department often found themselves united against a common enemy, the education boards. In some senses, indeed, a strong department is the result of the Institute's seeking central government protection for its members in the late nineteenth century against injustices at the hands of education boards and, occasionally, school committees, both often lacking professional expertise.

Increasingly, the department has accepted advice from the Institute and since 1924 has submitted all new regulations to it for comment. On many occasions the department has responded to Institute wishes. These good relations could also owe something to the fact that, until recently, many of the key positions in the department were occupied by ex-Institute office-holders. The most likely reason for the harmony, however, is that the Institute's executive rarely takes a very hard line in its negotiations with the department; if feasible it leaves room for manoeuvre and compromise after hearing the department's counter-arguments. Occasionally the executive, unable to reach agreement with the department, has gone directly to the Minister of Education, but such appeals are few in number (Ingle, 1967).

Institute officials are proud of their skill as negotiators and their role in shaping educational policy. 'The readiness of those in charge of educational administration,' said the president of the Institute in an address printed in its monthly journal, *National Education*, 'to consult and act in co-operation with teachers in introducing educational changes as indicative of the influence of our own teacher organizations' (Hawkins, 1960, 12). Again, two years later the journal's editor commented on the just published Report of the Commission on Education thus: 'We could not have said more; we could not have said it better. Page after page of the report is good Institute policy founded on years of experience' (Goodwin, 1962, 337). But a price has to be paid, and the Institute, in becoming in fact almost part of the hierarchy, has, in one critic's view, sacrificed effectiveness on the altar of respectability and become 'politically neutered' (Butterworth, 1968, 46). Such a judgment is provocative rather than accurate. But it is true that the Institute has in the postwar period acquired a high degree of respectability and a certain air of complacency.

In comparison, the Post-Primary Teachers' Association appears militant and unco-operative. This is not surprising for, since 1945, secondary education in New Zealand has undergone a revolution, the full consequences of which, many secondary teachers believe, have not been fully understood by Ministers of Education, departmental officers or the general public. The Post-Primary Teachers' Association leaders, as representatives of what was, for many years, an inadequately rewarded and unduly criticized branch of the teaching profession, have therefore spoken and acted in ways unlikely to endear them or their organization to the minister of the time and his senior departmental officers who have not concealed their displeasure at some utterances of the secondary teachers' spokesmen.

The association's skill and assurance as a negotiating body has not been helped by its recent origins and its diverse membership. Before 1952, when an act of union took place, there were two separate secondary teachers' organizations; the Secondary Schools' Association represented teachers who taught in 'academic' schools, and the Technical School Teachers' Association was for teachers in secondary technical schools. For all practical purposes, however, the distinction between academic and technical schools ceased to have meaning after the raising of the school-leaving age in 1945. Nevertheless, discussions about forming a single body for all secondary teachers led nowhere until the New Zealand Educational Institute invited technical teachers to join its ranks. Had this invitation been accepted, the Secondary Schools' Association might also have been forced to seek union. Instead, its executive immediately made ardent advances to the Technical School Teachers' Association and a single unified secondary teachers' organization, the Post-Primary Teachers' Association, was created.

Formed at a time of impending crisis in secondary education, the Post-Primary Teachers' Association soon ran into difficulties with the Department of Education. Members of the new alliance were reluctant to trust their executive to speak or act with real authority. Departmental officers did not like what they considered to be blatant 'pressure tactics' employed by the association's negotiators. And so a reputation for militancy and irascibility was acquired, although, in retrospect, it can now be argued that the association's belligerence was unavoidable in the circumstances of the 1950s and 1960s.

During those two decades, as the secondary school population expanded enormously, the Post-Primary Teachers' Association was forced into a difficult position. While constantly having to goad the department into action which would increase the numbers of men and women recruited into the secondary teaching service, it had also to try to ensure that the calibre of entrants was not lowered. The confrontations which have attracted greatest public attention between association and department, have been about salaries and salary scales. But the association has also wrangled for years about staffing ratios and the provision of ancillary staff. Relations reached their nadir in 1961 and 1962 over rates of payment for markers of the Department of Education's national fifth form examination, School Certificate. In the course of a prolonged and extraordinarily bitter clash the original cause of the dispute was almost completely lost sight of as misunderstanding followed misunderstanding.

Association members, believing the existence of their organization to be threatened, closed ranks as never before and prepared for a real trial of strength with the department. In the end, although not emerging as clear victors (the matter was resolved by independent arbitration), the association gained in stature and strength as a negotiating body. The regional branches agreed to give greater powers to their executive, and the department adopted a policy of more regular consultation with it (Ingle, 1967). Since 1963, with many of its struggles as a trade union behind it, the association has concerned itself much more with wider educational issues, especially the development of a more relevant curriculum. Its most ambitious effort was to set up its own curriculum review group whose perceptive report, *Curriculum in Change*, published in 1969, helped induce the department to initiate its own wide-ranging review of the secondary school curriculum, the first for twenty-nine years.

So directly do teachers' organizations affect the shaping of educational policy that it is sometimes said the New Zealand education system is one run by teachers for teachers. But such a facile summing up overlooks the fact that there still remain deeprooted differences of opinion between the Institute and the association, and that as long as these persist, the influence of teachers on policy formulation will be restricted. Co-operation and good fellowship, for example, evaporate when the Institute and the association discuss intermediate schools, and, to a lesser extent, district high schools and Form I to VI or VII schools. The association's view is that secondary education should begin at the first form level, not the third, a view opposed by the Institute which is determined to keep urban intermediate schools as part of the primary service. The two organizations also differ sharply on teacher-training: the Institute would prefer to see all recruits trained in the same institutions; the association's policy (which may be undergoing revision) has consistently been that all secondary teachers should be trained in separate secondary teachers' colleges.

Other professional interest groups

No one organization represents teachers in technical institutes, teachers' colleges and universities. Each group has its own association, but of the three only the Association of University Teachers, concerned to persuade the government to recognize the need for

42

some degree of parity between New Zealand and Australian university salaries, has ever acted as a real pressure group. In nearly forty centres in 1966 and 1967, when the government's openly expressed alarm at the sharply rising costs of education suggested possible retrenchment, Combined Educational Associations, representing all local interests, were formed to work for the good of education generally. The responsibility of the association's national committee was to keep before the government a balanced picture of educational needs. This committee claimed credit for persuading senior officials of Treasury and the Departments of Labour and Education of the need to integrate educational with social and economic planning so that education could make its optimum contribution to economic growth. Certainly, education was prominent among the terms of reference of the 1968 National Development Conference.

Pressures from outside the system

Since 1945, the only interest groups outside the system which have persistently pressured the government or the Department of Education have been rural or religious. They alone have succeeded in influencing to a significant degree the formulation of educational policy. Parents, the most immediately concerned interest group, although often vocal in their complaints about the shortcomings, real or imagined, of the particular schools their children attend, are seldom sufficiently organized. Their influence tends to be indirect and stems from their membership of local branches of the political parties or from criticism expressed through the Press. Occasionally such criticism, if sustained and trenchant, can compel the policy-makers to take notice. An example of what can be achieved was seen in 1958 when a parents' group, the Wellington Education Enquiry Association, attempted to persuade the Minister of Education to set in motion a full-scale, impartial investigation of the publicly controlled school system. The cautious compromise decided on by the minister, a study by senior inspectors of the standards of primary education in their districts, was rejected even before it was begun by the Education Enquiry Association and its editorial champions, who claimed it would only lead to more departmental whitewashing and to more papering over of the cracks in the educational edifice.

Criticism of primary education had reached a peak by 1958 but was not new; it had been growing ever since the abolition in 1936 of the primary-school leaving examination, Proficiency, which had allowed teachers more freedom to interpret the curriculum in terms of activity and experience. Teachers began, warily for a number of years, to spend less time on grammar, spelling, oral reading and formal arithmetic, and more on music, art and crafts, nature study and physical education. In so doing they were following, rather belatedly, a trend already well established in England and the United States but one which in New Zealand after 1945 filled many parents and businessmen with unease. Reassuring official statements failed to silence criticism (*A to J*, 1952, E–2, 4). Even the Minister of Education, R. M. Algie, soon after taking up office, seemed to doubt if the 3Rs were 'in their rightful place' in the primary school curriculum (Algie, 1950, 4). Although some of the criticism was justified, most of it, as a former Chief Inspector of Primary Schools in the 1950s has pointed out, sprang from a failure on the part of the public to appreciate that the changes being introduced in New Zealand primary schools were part of a general movement affecting all English-speaking countries (Ewing, 1970, 195), and did not lower the standards of achievement in the basic subjects.

Public discussion was at a highly emotional level; conservatives dubbed the work of the primary schools 'the playway'; some newspaper editors spoke in derogatory terms of New Zealand school children being 'led up the primrose path of Beebyism'. Parental anxiety was not allayed by press reports that apprentices could not pass their theory examinations because of their 'appallingly' low educational attainments, by newspaper headlines proclaiming 'Youth not equipped in fundamentals' or by newspaper correspondents who, with a plethora of comparative education data, could apparently prove that the New Zealand school system was one in which children learned 'the least possible in the longest possible time' (*Evening Post*, 10 April 1958).

In association with the New Zealand Council for Educational Research (a government-supported but independent research foundation and test development agency established in 1933), inspectors of the Department of Education, to compare achievement over the years and New Zealand standards with those of other countries, re-applied certain tests for which results were available from earlier surveys. The inquiry showed no significant change in the average standard of New Zealand twelve-year-olds in the basic skills of arithmetic, spelling and reading over the preceding thirty years but marked gains in reading for meaning and in oral English. New Zealand children were not very different from English and Australian in their grasp of the fundamental skills of arithmetic and spelling and reached a much higher standard in reading. Breadth had not been gained at the expense of basic skills.

Many parents, however, were not convinced by these findings when they were published early in 1959. This reaction did not surprise the Minister of Education and his senior departmental advisers who had already resigned themselves to the inevitability of constituting a Commission on Education to carry out an independent survey. Although the Minister of Education continued to deny it, doubtless the government was influenced by the activities of the Wellington Education Enquiry Association and similar bodies and by the overwhelming support given them by the press.

The attention such groups of parents received can be credited less to the sweeping accusations and generalizations they made than to the recognition in official circles that the opinions they expressed were symptomatic of a genuine and widespread concern, often bewilderment, about modern educational methods and trends. These parental pressure groups did not, however, continue to act as educational watchdogs; having secured their immediate objective, an impartial commission, they quietly faded away.

Other special interest groups have emerged from time to time seeking to reform a particular feature or supposed shortcoming of the school system. These groups are sometimes in advance of public opinion and seldom attract much attention, in large part because newspaper editors do not consider educational causes particularly newsworthy. And newspaper crusades are rare in New Zealand. Certainly few editors are prepared to help groups whose values or attitudes conflict with those of the community at large, and are thus unlikely to attract much public sympathy.

There was, for example, very sparse press coverage given in 1969 to the efforts of a group of citizens who petitioned parliament to have corporal punishment banned in infant classes and fifth and sixth forms. (This had been a recommendation of the Commission on Education seven years earlier.) The petition was referred to a Select Committee of the House on Education which, in a series of protracted hearings, gathered together a great deal of evidence including a Department of Education statement which made it clear that officially the retention of corporal punishment in schools was not favoured and that its frequent use was 'rightly regarded as a sign of professional incompetence'. The committee's eventual recommendation to the House, however, was that the petition be 'favourably received' rather than, as the petitioners had hoped, that it be 'most favourably received'.

The press showed little interest in the public hearings when the petitioners presented carefully-documented evidence to support the abolition of corporal punishment. Journalists know that many adult New Zealanders, especially the men, see nothing wrong with the continued use of corporal punishment, at least in the secondary schools. There is widespread respect for the use of physical force in the community and physical toughness and manliness are often equated (both on and off the rugby field). In any case, discipline within New Zealand homes is not unseldom heavy, arbitrary and unreflective; teachers and classrooms merely mirror the values and attitudes of the homes.

PART TWO

Major social issues

PART TWO

4

Church and state in education

Religious teaching in state schools

The contemporary New Zealand education system bears clear traces of its nineteenth-century English and Scottish origins. But like much of the fauna and flora introduced at the same time, it now has its own characteristics. A main difference, one that has caused much argument, is the secularity of New Zealand primary education. When the state took control of education in 1877 it adopted a policy of neutrality; it 'deliberately refrained from teaching religion and also from supporting religious teachings by grants from public funds' (Commission on Education, 1962, 676).

This decision was not taken lightly. At the beginning of the debates on the 1877 Education Bill a majority of members of the General Assembly favoured some form of religious instruction. In the first draft of the Bill a clause was included which proposed that the school day should open with the Lord's Prayer and a reading from the Bible. When, however, it appeared that the passage of much-needed legislation was in danger because of this clause a few Members of the House of Representatives, the lower house, met secretly, it is said, and pledged themselves to vote for a secular clause. After the longest debate in New Zealand parliamentary history the draft proposal was struck out and was replaced by the clause which, repeated in the 1914 and 1964 Education Acts, has ensured the continuing secularity of the national primary system: 'The school shall be kept open 5 days in each week for at least 4 hours in each day, 2 of which in the forenoon and 2 in the afternoon shall be consecutive and the teaching shall be of a secular character.'

The passage into law of this clause soon brought into being the first of many groups prepared to campaign actively to have the law changed. In 1879, Presbyterians in Otago and Southland began to agitate against the offending clause, with the result that a petition was presented to parliament in 1880 praying that the Education Act be

49

amended to allow Bible reading in public schools. This petition's lack of success was repeated in 1885, when a private member's Bill with the same objective, the first of 42 such Bills initiated in the course of the next half century, was rejected by parliament. The churches did not try to bring pressure to bear on the government until 1903, when, at an inter-church conference, they decided to form a Bible-in-Schools League, whose aim was to have the Act amended. But well organized and led as the League often was, it never quite succeeded. In part this was because the Education Act of 1877 had come to be regarded as something almost sacrosanct, in part because New Zealand politicians have always been wary of becoming embroiled in sectarian strife.

The league's proposals changed over the years. Before the Second World War it wanted state teachers to give one thirty-minute Bible lesson daily. The league's spokesmen claimed that they were not asking that teachers teach religion, but merely that they ensured children understood Bible lessons as intelligently as other lessons. After 1918, the league increasingly attempted to extend to primary schools the system of opening school each day with devotional exercises like those permitted in state secondary schools, and argued that it was simply trying to make the national system self-consistent.

Because the 1877 Education Act referred only to state public schools (by definition primary and district high schools) the secular clause did not apply to secondary schools, which at that time were established by their own Acts of Parliament. No provision has since been made to alter this rather anomalous situation, on which the Commission on Education commented: 'It may be confidently asserted that this was not due to any general view of the appropriateness of secular instruction for primary pupils as against secondary. It was an historical accident' (Commission on Education, 1962, 677). Religious instruction in state secondary schools is entirely at the discretion of the controlling authorities. In fact, it rarely goes beyond that which the Bible-in-Schools League sought in the 1920s, the beginning of each school day with a hymn, a Bible reading and a prayer.

In public schools neither the league's pre-war nor its post-war proposals were adopted. The churches, by this time, were divided among themselves about the league's policy. Preferring some progress to none, many churchmen looked with growing favour on the 'Nelson system', a scheme for providing religious instruction in primary schools without amending the secular clause. Bible-in-Schools League stalwarts scorned the Nelson system, claiming that it was tantamount 'to slinking in by the back door'.

In a very real sense, they were right; while the Bible-in-Schools League supporters sought legislative change, advocates of the Nelson system were content to make use of loopholes in the 1877 Act, loopholes which were not closed by the consolidating Education Act of 1914. Clause 84, subsection 2 of the 1877 Act, which laid down that schools be open for at least two hours each morning and two each afternoon, was followed by a subsection which left it to the discretion of local school committees to decide what use should be made of school buildings when schools were not officially in session. In another section of the 1877 Act permission was given to the education board of each district to define the opening and closing times of primary schools. After careful study of these provisions, a Presbyterian minister in Nelson, the Rev. J. H. McKenzie, concluded, what a Dunedin newspaper editor had suggested in 1878, that there was a way round the secular clause. In 1897 he persuaded the Nelson Education Board to reduce the customary school day from five hours to four-and-a-half on one day a week so that religious instruction could be given legitimately in the first half hour of a normal school day by not declaring the school open until the end of a period of religious instruction taken by outside teachers (usually local Protestant clergy).

Apart from its apparent legality, the outstanding advantage of this scheme, in the eyes of its advocates, was that almost all the children were present at religious instruction, although parents, of course, had the right to withdraw them. The legality of McKenzie's manoeuvre was eventually challenged on the grounds that education boards did not have the power to validate, through their by-laws, the reduced hours of secular instruction, but this point was never tested in law and the Nelson system gained some ground. Its popularity before the Second World War was never great, however, although the proportion of schools using it did increase, especially in Otago, from the 10 per cent known to have been following the Nelson example in 1930.

The apathy of many clergymen, denominational rivalry, distance between country schools, local resistance or unconcern all accounted for its limited acceptance. It was also feared that, if the Nelson system won general favour, the Catholic Church's case for grants-in-aid of its own widespread system of primary and secondary schools would become irresistible. And if grants-in-aid to Catholic schools were approved, it would be very difficult to withhold similar grants from other religious bodies or private groups wishing to expand or establish their own schools.

Religious teaching since 1945

In 1949 a new body, the New Zealand Council for Christian Education, was created to replace the moribund Bible-in-Schools League. This council became the spokesman for all Protestant groups seeking to have religious instruction made a regular and legitimate part of the primary school curriculum. The churches wanted a place for religion in the schools because enrolments in the Sunday schools were declining. Indeed, Sunday schools were not able to meet the need to provide religious and moral training for the young. A curriculum that was increasingly dated, teachers unable to inspire interest and an increasing number of week-end counter-attractions combined to make their task impossible. The New Zealand Council for Christian Education realized, like the Bible-in-Schools League, that to ensure that the fundamentals of Christian doctrine were taught to large numbers of children its teachers had to win greater access to the public schools. The council's task was made easier by the decline in denominationalism after 1945 as a result of the ecumenical movement. This changed climate meant that in 1950 the council could devise an agreed syllabus along English lines and train a corps of voluntary instructors drawn from different denominations.

With better qualified instructors, the council exploited the possibilities of the Nelson system more fully. By 1960 it claimed that the Nelson system was in use in 80 per cent of the country's primary schools. But it was still not satisfied that its instructors were making any major cultural or educational contributions to the lives of the children. Like many of their class teachers, the children too often looked upon the weekly half-hour of religious instruction as an irrelevant but not unwelcome break in regular school routine.

The New Zealand Council for Christian Education's dissatisaction with the Nelson system was heightened by its awareness that by making greater use of it, the council was often condoning illegal practices, that it was indeed 'slinking in by the back door'. In many districts the whole school assembled before the religious instruction class was held; while the religious teacher was taking his lesson other classes were doing their normal school work; religious instruction was being permitted during a time which interrupted the two consecutive hours of secular instruction laid down by the Act in morning and afternoon. And yet these practices were inevitable if effective use was to be made of the council's two thousand or so voluntary instructors.

In some education board districts these irregularities were of such long standing that they had come to be accepted as customary and normal; other education boards, however, attempted to enforce strict legality. 'During the last few years,' the New Zealand Council for Christian Education stated in its submission to the Commission on Education, 'the Council's work has been made more difficult by the enforcement in some places of a strict and rigid interpretation of the Nelson system.' The council sought to persuade the commission to recommend a change in the law to permit legally what had long been done illegally.

The commissioners were sympathetic because their inquiries showed fairly general satisfaction with the operation of the Nelson system. They agreed that there were 'good grounds for recommending such an amendment to the Act as expressing the will of the majority' (Commission on Education, 1962, 680), adding, however, that they were unanimous in reaffirming 'the secular principle in New Zealand primary school education, understanding by that principle the exclusion from the officially prescribed primary school curriculum of any instruction in the tenets of any religion or sect' (Commission on Education, 1962, 685). In its final recommendations the commission made two further important points: first, that no state primary teacher should be permitted to give religious instruction on school premises during the school week, and second, that every parent or guardian of a child entering primary school be required to sign a brief statement declaring whether or not he wished his child to be given religious instruction by voluntary instructors during school hours.

The commission's recommendations went only part way towards

meeting the wishes of the New Zealand Council for Christian Education. Many churchmen claimed that large numbers of primary school teachers were anxious to take religious instruction and that the law should be appropriately amended. The Minister of Education of the day, Blair Tennent, was clearly influenced by these and other arguments when he drafted the Religious Instruction and Observances in Public Schools Act in 1962. This Act, consolidated in the 1964 Education Act, provided that where a public school committee, after consultation with the principal, so determined, 'any class or classes at the school, or the school as a whole, might be closed at any time or times of the school day for a period not exceeding thirty minutes for any class in any week for religious instruction and religious observances or for either of these' (*A to J*, 1963, E–1, 6). Religious instruction at such times was to be given by voluntary instructors approved by the school committee and religious observances were to be conducted in a manner also approved by the committee. The Act further provided that no pupil was to attend religious instruction or observances if his parent or guardian objected in writing. In addition, the Act set out the circumstances in which teachers might be freed from their duties to take part in religious instruction and observances in their own schools.

The passage of this Act was a major victory for the religious interest groups, made the more remarkable because it was won in the face of the most determined opposition from the New Zealand Educational Institute. The prophecy made in 1913 by a Bible-in-Schools League leader, 'Victory awaits us: the cause of God cannot be defeated,' appeared to have come true.

The elation of the Act's supporters was matched by the gloom of its opponents. One member of parliament declared that the proposed legislation was a fundamental breach of the Education Act, which could well wreck the whole state system. In particular, he and other critics objected that the two riders of the commission had been flouted, namely that no state primary school teachers should take part in religious instruction and that children should 'contract in' to it. The Act, however, required children to 'contract out' and allowed teachers to give religious instruction in their own schools.

The second of these provisions particularly dismayed a great many people, not just the Institute. They objected that if public school teachers gave religious instruction, then no matter how it is argued, it would be at public expense. Then the question becomes intimately and indissolubly connected with public financial support for church schools. Significantly, members of parliament on both sides of the House chose not to debate this issue.

The victory, although it seemed major in 1962, has not been as substantial as was anticipated—or feared. Fewer than two hundred state teachers have chosen to teach religion in their own schools; the New Zealand Council for Christian Education has had difficulty in maintaining agreement among all its members about the syllabus to be followed and there is evidence that some voluntary teachers use their lessons to proselytize and to propagate sectarian ideas. If it appeared that such a practice had become widespread, public anti-pathy to the present arrangements about religious instruction would be aroused; the New Zealand public are, as the Commission on Education observed, 'still much concerned to protect their children from the inconsiderate zealot' (Commission on Education, 1962, 684).

The 1962 Religious Instruction and Observances in Public Schools Act has not proved the panacea advocates of religious instruction had hoped. 'Neither religiously nor educationally,' one theologian has written, 'can this be called a wholly satisfactory situation. Much remains to be improved . . . if pupils are not to regard [their religious instruction] as a waste of time, rather than the result of a long struggle to resolve the competing claims of church and state in education in a way which does not unduly threaten liberty of conscience for teacher or child' (Breward, 1967, 99).

The task of the New Zealand Council for Christian Education has been further complicated by the influx of Catholic children to form sizeable minorities in state primary schools. The council's agreed syllabus had not taken this possibility into account. Should an attempt be made anywhere to separate the Catholic minority from the rest for religious instruction, other sects which do not belong to the council would seek the same privilege.

The state aid to private schools controversy

Few New Zealanders seriously believe that the concessions granted to Protestants seeking to introduce religious teaching into state primary schools constitute a 'fundamental breach' of the public and secular nature of the system. Many people, however, fear that the apparent readiness of governments since the early 1960s to increase financial aid to private schools will lead to such a breach. Opposition to any increase in grants-in-aid to sectarian schools stems partly from a generally held belief that they should be self-supporting and partly from an antipathy towards anything which smacks, however faintly, of privilege.

The state aid issue in New Zealand educational politics, although very much to the fore since 1945, is older than the national system itself, going back to the provincial period (1852–76) when a number of provincial governments financially supported church-controlled school systems. The experience was not particularly happy and in the five years or so immediately prior to the Abolition of the Provinces Act in 1876 the trend in all the provinces was away from church control. Schools everywhere were becoming public and secular. In introducing his Education Bill in 1877 the Minister of Justice, Charles Bowen, summed up provincial experience when he said (*NZPD*, 1877, vol. 24, 36):

> It has been found that wherever an attempt has been made to divide among the religious bodies the money raised for educational purposes the funds have been frittered away; that small inferior schools have been kept up instead of large efficient schools being established by a concentrated effort on the part of the state and that there was always difficulty in obtaining the money which was absolutely required for the maintenance of an educational system.

After lengthy and heated discussions, with Catholic members of both the Legislative Council and the House of Representatives fighting determined rearguard actions all the way, one nationally financed and publicly-controlled primary school system was established for the mass of the children of the colony. The creation of a dual system along the lines established in England and Wales by the Elementary Education Act of 1870 was considered and deliberately rejected. 'The Education Act of 1877,' the Report of the Commission on Education comments, 'marks the rejection by the state, in the name of the New Zealand political community, of any form of financial or administrative partnership between the state and the religious denominations in the field of public education' (Commission on Education, 1962, 710).

Growth of the private sector

The Protestant and Catholic Churches reacted differently to the Act's denial of financial aid to denominational schools. The Protestants allowed their schools to become part of the public system and concentrated on amending the Act to permit religious instruction in state schools. The Catholics, to whom the secular nature of the 1877 Act was even more repugnant, immediately set about building-up, on a diocesan basis, their own voluntarily-financed system of primary schools.

During the next fifty years the number of private primary schools, mostly Catholic, grew rapidly. In 1969 three-quarters of the country's 344 private primary schools were Catholic. Even so, Catholic authorities are unable to meet the demand for places. In the early 1970s over 40 per cent of Catholic children of primary school age were attending public schools. In 1969 private primary schools catered for 11 per cent of the age cohort and private secondary schools for 15 per cent. In both cases these percentages were slightly lower than in 1945.

A few non-Catholic private primary schools, established because of parental dissatisfaction with local state schools, are 'progressive' but, in general, private schools, primary and secondary, are very conventional. This is not surprising in the case of the secondary schools because the English 'public schools', whose organization and style many of them follow so assiduously, have themselves 'never stood for a particular form of learning but for a particular form of environment' (Baron, 1965, 137). Nevertheless, when the state system is so uniform, it is unfortunate that the private schools should follow the state schools so closely. The national curriculum is taught in almost all private schools and the secondary schools enter pupils for national examinations. Moreover they are inhibited because they must be registered with the Department of Education and be open to regular inspection. Many private secondary schools do differ, however, in one respect; they were originally founded to educate Christians. Religious studies and observance occupy a central place in all Catholic schools, for example, and Anglican schools for boys and girls—nearly all private secondary schools are single-sex—seek to develop their life around the chapel.

The non-Catholic private secondary schools and their associated preparatory departments charge high tuition fees and thus tend to be socially exclusive. A sociologist has calculated that, in one old-established Anglican boys' school from 1918 to 1968, only 1 per cent of the boys enrolled came from working- and lower middle-class homes (Vellekoop, 1968). The belief that the non-Catholic private secondary schools are socially divisive in that they accentuate the economic and occupational backgrounds of their pupils is not without substance, and largely explains the public outcry whenever the government increases financial aid to the private sector.

Pressure for aid

The 1877 settlement rejecting any form of financial or administrative partnership in education between the state and the churches remained intact for almost seventy years, although Catholic leaders never ceased to object to the exclusion from financial aid of their school system which, they argued, they were in conscience bound to provide. Quite apart from the fear of re-awakening or exacerbating sectarian bitterness—a brooding suspicion of the Catholic Church has long been a characteristic of New Zealand society—no political party was prepared to test the substance of the contention widely expressed by prominent New Zealand educators that the very existence of the state school system would be threatened by government support for church-controlled schools. Some anti-state-aiders went further and argued that the whole fabric of New Zealand society depended upon the maintenance of a single public school system. This widely held view was echoed in a submission by the New Zealand Educational Institute to the commission. If state assistance were given to competing school systems, the Institute averred, education would become 'a divisive rather than a unifying factor in our life with all the consequent evils in the social and econ-omic structure resulting from over-emphasis of the sectarian factor'.

The state aid issue, dormant for so long, flared up in the immediate post-war years when greatly increased enrolments created acute staffing difficulties for Catholic schools and left them with insufficient and inadequate buildings. Catholic hopes of state aid had been heightened by the announcement at the Christchurch Ministerial Conference on Education in 1944 of additional assistance (depart-mental publications, free milk and boarding allowances) to Catholic and other private school pupils. These concessions, together with a very cautious remark made by the minister about the place in New Zealand of private schools, 'I welcome the diversity that schools independent of the state are capable of introducing,' encouraged Catholic educational authorities to believe that at last a government was going to treat their case sympathetically. Their hopes soared higher when their spokesman, the Rev. Dr N. H. Gascoigne, was invited to put the case for state aid to private schools before the caucus of the Labour Party (then the government) in 1948. Somewhat emotionally he rehearsed many of the arguments which have been used constantly since: Catholic parents were paying twice over for the education of their children; Catholic children were being denied the equality of educational opportunity promised by Peter Fraser in 1939; not only were they not being given a fair deal but in many ways they were being actively discriminated against. 'Only last week,' said Dr Gascoigne, 'my eyes saw this, a by-product of the 1877 Act. . . . I beheld little New Zealand children walking the roads of this country; I saw state school buses swirl them with dust, aboard those buses other little New Zealand children, and the ones who walked the roads going to a school where they would be taught to love everyone, yes, the ones in the buses that passed them.'

If the politicians' hearts had been touched by Dr Gascoigne's plea for justice there was little indication of it in the actions of the Labour Government in its last year in office, although Prime Minister Peter Fraser did make one apparently minor concession which in the long run proved to be a major one. He personally authorized subsidies on film projectors for Catholic schools. After this it was but a short step to subsidizing all equipment bought by private schools on the same basis as for state schools. The succeeding National Government seemed unwilling to make further concessions even though it was clear that many Catholic schools were in dire financial straits. In exasperation Archbishop McKeefry of Wellington said:

In the matter of our schools, we are only asking for justice. . . . We are tired of being fobbed off and I say that, should war come, and if it is to be fought overseas, then my thought at the moment is that I should feel inclined to call on our men to stay at home whilst those who deny us justice here can do the fighting overseas (*Dominion*, 16 November 1954).

59

At about this time the Holy Name Society, an organization which campaigned vigorously for state aid throughout the 1950s, began to apply direct pressure on the politicians. In a letter to the prime minister, the society claimed that in the previous elections many Catholic voters had voted for a minor party's candidates rather than for his because that party promised justice for private schools. The Holy Name Society asked that a Parliamentary Committee of Inquiry be set up. When, after a long delay, the government showed no signs of acceding to its request, the society decided to petition parliament directly 'for such changes in the law as will make financial assistance available to private schools'.

While the petition was in preparation, considerable emotional heat was engendered; the heavy-handed, militant approach of the organizers offended many, including the Minister of Education. There was, however, very thorough public discussion of all facets of the state aid question before the society finally presented its petition in September 1956.

The opponents of state aid rallied their forces. A succession of witnesses who appeared before the Select Committee on Education countered the Catholic arguments for financial support. Having heard much evidence the Select Committee recommended that no action be taken on the grounds that to grant the petition would seem to set aside the traditional principle of the separation of church and state; second, that the organizations representing state educational interests were convinced that it would be tantamount to destroying the public school system as many other groups would soon seek state aid; and third, that the weight of evidence given before the committee suggested general satisfaction with existing educational arrangements (*NZPD*, 1956, vol. 310, 27).

Discomforted but not defeated, the Catholic educational interest groups withdrew to prepare for the next round. They now looked critically at their own existing educational arrangements, especially at the sweeping powers parish priests had over their schools, and admitted that there was need for reform. Worthwhile reforms would be too costly for the Catholic Church and parishioners to undertake without state assistance, so once again the Catholic pressure groups were forced to the attack. They took advantage of the fact that the state secondary schools were hard pressed to cater for the post-war population bulge by threatening to restrict entry to their secondary schools. Another tactic was tried when the national president of the Holy Name Society called on Catholics to cast aside political affiliations at the next general election and to 'vote for the man . . . with principles and integrity who would see the justice of the cause of state aid for private schools' (Chapman, Jackson and Mitchell, 1962, 103).

These efforts were, as it happened, largely wasted. The government dodged the issue by asking the Commission on Education which it had just set up to recommend a policy with regard to state assistance to private schools. The commission did not welcome its task, a fact it made clear in its report. 'The Commission feels constrained,' ran the opening paragraph of the chapter on state aid, 'to state from the beginning that the ultimate resolution of this problem . . . is to be found rather within the realms of politics and of community attitude and belief than of pure logic or educational theory' (Commission on Education, 1962, 698).

All the politicians knew the commission was right, but in a general election year all were glad to see the topic removed, even if only temporarily, from the realm of practical politics. On this score at least there was remarkable unanimity among them.

The commission hearing

The commission received in all forty-five separate submissions on the question of state aid. These submissions fell into three clearly distinguishable groups.

The first, made up entirely of submissions from Catholic organizations and from Catholic citizens, sought direct financial assistance for private schools from public funds. The second group consisted of submissions from the controlling authorities of Protestant independent schools and a few other organizations; these sought subsidies on equipment and tax relief for parents who educated their children privately. The third, and by far the largest group of submissions, came mainly from education boards, the primary and secondary teachers' organizations and from members of school committees, parent–teacher associations and home and school associations. These unanimously advocated no additional financial assistance.

In the end, the commission concluded that it could not 'recommend a change in public policy in this matter' (Commission on Education, 1962, 716). Although the conclusion bitterly disappointed Catholic educational interest groups, it was not unexpected. Their opponents had argued their case with well practised ease before a commission which included one member who, in 1956, when opposing the petition of the Holy Name Society, had expressed 'emphatic opposition to the proposition that public grants-in-aid or tax exemption be accorded to groups or individuals in respect of non-State schools'.

The state aid question in the 1960s

Having failed in two sustained and determined bids to secure greater financial assistance for their schools, the Catholic pressure groups adopted gentler tactics in the 1960s. No major campaigns were mounted; instead every opportunity was taken to emphasize the simple justice of their case, the healthy partnership which had developed between state and independent schools—the terms 'private' and 'church' became less and less frequently used—and the great saving to the state which resulted from the existence of non-state schools.

For its part the government was now more willing than earlier governments to brave the wrath of other educational pressure groups by making concessions to the independent schools. It heeded the advice of the Commission on Education and treated the state aid issue as a political, rather than an educational, problem. It ignored the commission's advice, however, when in 1962 it followed the precedent set by the Commonwealth Government in Australia in 1952 and allowed limited relief from personal taxation for expenses incurred in the purchase of a private school education

This concession, which was in line with proposals made by the Associated Chambers of Commerce of New Zealand and the Federated Farmers of New Zealand, was to some extent prompted by concern for the financially straitened Protestant secondary schools rather than by a sudden appreciation of the plight of the Catholic schools. The governing bodies of many of these non-Catholic schools, stretched to the limit of their financial resources, abandoned their former aloof attitude to state aid and in 1962 made common cause with Catholic educational interests in the Interdenominational Committee of Independent Schools. This committee then approached the government for assistance and was rewarded in 1963 with a major grant. Further substantial grants were made in 1966 and 1968.

These grants were consistent with the declared intention of the National Government throughout the 1960s to reach 'a satisfactory and equitable solution of the controversial question of state assistance to independent schools'. Its solution was not novel; clearly yielding to pressure from the independent schools—including a threat by the chairman of the Catholic Educational Council for New Zealand to send all Catholic children up to standard four to the state schools—the government took the simple way out by giving more money. In defence of this solution, the Minister of Education used the hoary and fallible argument so often advanced in favour of state aid that the government, while recognizing the need to spend more on the state system, 'was mindful of the fact that if private schools did not continue in existence the resulting heavy increase in government expenditure would make further developments in the state system more difficult to attain' (*Evening Post*, 4 December 1968).

The disappearance of rivalry between the Catholic and Protestant independent school interests has significantly altered the state aid situation. This fact, together with the diminution of sectarian bitterness and hostility in the community generally—a by-product of common schooling, those opposed to state aid would argue—will make it easier for future governments to increase state aid.

And there is no doubt that further aid will be given. The Labour and Social Credit parties during the 1969 general election campaign offered increased financial assistance while the Minister of Finance, a member of the cabinet's education committee, repeated an earlier remark by the Minister of Education that a National Government would not allow the independent schools to decline and disappear for financial reasons. ' "Sympathetic" negotiations will continue with the National Independent Schools' Committee,' he said. A promise made by the National Party during the 1969 election campaign was fulfilled in February 1970, when a Joint Cabinet-Caucus Committee on State Aid for Independent Schools was set up, not only to consider the Committee of Independent Schools' case, but also to consult all other persons or organizations which might wish to make representations. The committee, which did not report until ten months later, recommended, and the government agreed, that state financial assistance be increased from $1,100,000 a year to $2,500,000 as from 1 February 1970, and that further specified percentage increases be provided for over a seven-year period.

Whatever the precise nature of future aid—and it seems likely to be in the form of cheap loans, assistance with teacher training, capitation grants, or the part-payment of teachers' salaries—certain issues will create difficulties for any government. What control, for example, will the department exercise over the non-state schools? Will these schools, in fact, really be independent? Who will appoint the teachers? How will the government decide which schools deserve greater support and which do not? How can it distinguish between a fair deal for all the country's children and favouring a few? Have the separate issues of sectarianism and privilege become inextricably intertwined? Will it be possible to prevent the proliferation of private schools in areas where a single school would suffice? Could the final solution be that private schools will integrate into the state system as in Scotland and as a number of Maori denominational secondary schools did at the beginning of 1973?

Since financial assistance has already been granted fairly generously, all these and many other questions will need to be answered by future governments. Early in 1973 the Minister of Education in the third Labour Government promised to chair a full-scale inquiry into all aspects of the state aid issue which, he predicted, would settle the matter 'once and for all'. To restrict aid will prove an extremely difficult task. Nevertheless, the New Zealand school system remains essentially a public one and is likely to be so as long as the representatives of teaching organizations and the controlling authorities maintain their present vigilance. The general public, too, is prepared to countenance so much, and no more, assistance to private schools, some of which have earned the reputation of being 'snob' institutions. Most New Zealanders accept that there is a place for private schools—if only to provide for 'difficult' children or children of 'difficult' parents—but they believe that parents who want schooling beyond what the state offers should pay for it. New Zealanders do not want to see the Australian pattern introduced where state schools and state supported independent schools operate side by side, always to the disadvantage of the former. Under such an arrangement, said a past-president of the Post-Primary Teachers' Association, 'With all the children of the caring, the striving, the ambitious, the well-to-do parents in the private schools, no one will care about state education at all' (*Evening Post*, 2 October 1969).

5

Schooling in town and country

To ensure equality of educational opportunity for rural children has always been a major problem. Since the beginnings of the national system in 1877, the farmers have made sure that the educational interests of their children are kept well to the fore, a relatively easy task because of the political importance of the rural community. Parliamentary representatives from rural constituencies, many of whom probably cut their political teeth on school committee, governing body or education board work, try to ensure during discussions on educational expenditure that the needs of country children are not overlooked. They appreciate the point made by the Commission on Education that for parents in country districts 'the education of their children is a major preoccupation and even source of anxiety' (Commission on Education, 1962, 438).

At the primary stage there is little disparity between rural and urban educational opportunity and little difference in educational attainments. Because it has been deliberate government policy since 1939 to ensure that the country child is 'given access to the facilities from which he has always tended to be barred by the mere accident of location' (*A to J*, 1939, E–1, 7), the Director of Education, referring particularly to primary education, was able to claim in 1960 that New Zealand has 'evened up opportunities between town and country to a degree that is probably not exceeded anywhere else in the world, and in fact only very rarely approached' (Campbell, 1960, 4). In 1969 the rural primary school was lauded by the retiring Minister of Education as 'the gem in our educational system' (*Evening Post*, 10 December 1969).

The evenness of educational coverage in New Zealand, where about half the 2,200 public primary schools in 1971 were one-, two-, three- or four-classroom country schools, has been brought about in a number of ways. Country primary schools get the same equipment and similar supervisory assistance as urban schools. Promotion beyond a certain point on salary scales is possible only if the teacher

66

has taught for a specified period in country schools. The primary teachers' colleges give all students training and practice in the complexities of running a small school.

More important than any other factor in ensuring equality of educational opportunity for country children has been the practice of bringing children by bus from outlying districts to centrally located schools. As a result, the percentage of one-teacher or 'sole-charge' schools in the primary service had fallen from a peak of 60 per cent in 1927 to 13·4 per cent in 1970 and the Department of Education had become the operator of the second largest transport service in New Zealand.

For children living beyond the reach of the school bus, on high country farms, at lighthouses, beside remote bays, in roadless fiord country or unable to attend school because of illness or physical handicap, the Department of Education has since 1922 developed a very effective Correspondence School, whose pupils, both primary and secondary, as far as possible follow the same curriculum as other children, including practical work in art and crafts and science. Daily radio lessons supplement written materials and assignments. In addition, teachers from the Correspondence School in Wellington visit pupils' homes in the first term each year, while in certain areas itinerant 'resident teachers' call regularly on Correspondence School pupils in their districts. Special week-long courses for candidates for national examinations are organized from time to time. In November each year a four-week residential school for about forty girls or boys is held at a convenient centre to give children, whose schooling has been entirely by mail and radio, an opportunity to experience classroom and group activities, sporting and cultural as well as academic, and to receive special tuition in subjects not easily handled by correspondence. Correspondence School materials and services are available to any secondary school which finds itself temporarily short of staff but country secondary schools not infrequently need permanent help from the Correspondence School for groups of pupils taking specialist subjects such as Maori or physics.

Satisfaction with rural secondary education is not so general. Indeed, the limited nature of much rural secondary schooling probably contributes to the urban drift and the subsequent serious loss of skilled agricultural labour. The Department of Education which already spends, in terms of the number of children affected, a disproportionate amount on rural education, rebuts charges that it treats pupils in country high schools as second-class citizens by pointing out that all-age district high schools, the particular target for criticism, get the same per capita grants as other secondary schools. But this does not necessarily produce equal facilities or opportunities because secondary departments of district high schools are usually too small to qualify for adequate funds. To provide senior pupils with reasonable opportunities for specialization according to their interests and abilities the district high schools need larger per capita grants and better teaching and administrative facilities. Although district high schools now enrol a very much smaller percentage of the secondary school population than they did—3 per cent in 1970 compared with 18 per cent in 1945—and their numbers dropped in the same period from 104 to 63, there is still a place for them in the school system. Geographical factors in many parts of New Zealand prevent the amalgamation of small units to form better-sized secondary schools.

Wherever possible the government decided early in the 1960s to create larger units or 'composite schools' as they were called in the 1964 Education Act. These, it was hoped, would attract more teachers who between them would be able to teach a much wider range of subjects than was possible in a district high school. By 1971, despite the opposition of the New Zealand Educational Institute to the incorporation of Forms I and II in the secondary stage, this policy had led to the development of two new types of rural schools, the Form I–VI or VII high school and the area school, formed by adding the two senior classes from all the primary schools in an area to the secondary department of an existing district high school. The first of these schools had a secondary enrolment of only 81.

Staffing difficulties continue to hinder the work of all country secondary schools. Post-Primary Teachers' Association surveys have consistently shown that such schools have the lowest proportion of properly qualified staff and that the number of positions unfilled is well above the national average in spite of the 'country service regulations' (introduced in 1949 and amended from time to time since) which, with exceptions, make it impossible for secondary, like primary, teachers to advance beyond a certain step on the salary scale unless they have served or are serving a period—usually three years—in a country school. If a particular course or subject is not taught locally a country child is entitled to a boarding allowance to attend an urban secondary school, a number of which maintain hostels largely for such children. But still in the late 1960s the Post-Primary Teachers' Association claimed that rural children were the nation's educationally underprivileged.

Urbanization, a new problem

While the Department of Education concentrated on improving rural education it overlooked the seriousness of the difficulties, social as well as educational, besetting some urban schools. This oversight was understandable; traditionally, urban schools had rarely been a cause for concern, and urbanization, with its accompanying social complexities, is a comparatively new phenomenon in New Zealand but increasingly is a factor educational policy-makers will have to take into account. It has been predicted that, by 1986, only 28 per cent of the population will live outside seventeen major conurbations, the likely characteristics of which are already becoming apparent in Auckland and Wellington.

Each of these cities now has a declining inner-urban core; around the core is a stable ring of settlement where the rate of population growth is slowing down; beyond this again there is an outer ring which is constantly expanding. Although most New Zealanders are loath to speak in terms of social class, these three zones of settlement and the schools characteristic of them reflect the differences, acknowledged or unacknowledged, of incipient social stratification.

The inner city schools are like similar schools in Australian and North American cities; old, inconvenient, lacking in facilities and unattractive to teachers. They are attended in large numbers by children whose parents have just migrated from the country, from the Pacific Islands or from Europe. In Wellington in 1968, 70 per cent of the children on the roll of one city school were from racial minority groups. Maintenance of these schools is often neglected because of pressure on the education boards to provide new schools in the expanding suburbs. Parental support for the city schools varies but seldom approaches that consistently given to schools and their teachers in the middle ring of settlement inhabited by many well established middle-class New Zealanders. In the outer ring, the new housing areas, school buildings may look similar to those of the middle ring, but there the similarity ends. Schools in new suburbs are not so stable. Enrolments increase with unpredictable speed as more houses are finished and young couples move in. Families also frequently move out of these areas quite soon so that there is a high turnover rate among the pupils, matched, unfortunately, by that of the staff.

TABLE I   Rural–urban drift, 1926–71

| Census | % urban residents* | | Total number | |
	Maori	Pakeha	Maori	Pakeha
1926	15	69	64	1,337
1951	29	76	116	1,818
1956	35	77	137	2,033
1961	46	78	167	2,262
1966	61	80	201	2,505
1971	70	83	227	2,630

* Urban population defined as population in the 24 'Urban areas' plus towns with population 1,000 or over.

Many of the troubles experienced by these schools originate, of course, in the homes from which the children come. 'In a large number of cases,' said a delegate to the New Zealand Educational Institute's annual conference in 1969, 'we get children coming to school without being able to speak English; many come with no pre-school training; some come with no moral standards whatsoever' (*Evening Post*, 15 May 1969). In such circumstances the schools should be trying to help the community but they have insufficient resources. Neither have guidelines been laid down for the schools to follow. The Commission on Education, in a chapter entitled 'School Buildings and their Community Use', wrote approvingly but vaguely of schools becoming community centres. Elsewhere it recommended that schools in decaying urban or new housing areas should be given improved staffing schedules. Apart from these general recommendations it did not try to suggest solutions for what has been described as 'the most serious and urgent problem in New Zealand education today' (*Evening Post*, 15 May 1969).

So grave has this situation become, indeed, that if the New

Zealand Government through its Department of Education is to fulfil its guarantee of full equality of educational opportunity for all, positive and substantial measures must be taken to aid the under-privileged children living in areas which are tending to become, certainly in the popular view if not yet in fact, the nation's social black spots. Teachers should be provided with low rental housing in the districts where they teach so that they may serve as a stabiliz-ing element. Some of them should be paid extra to supervise children's recreational activities out of school hours. New schools in the new housing areas should be better equipped than is presently the case. The government's 1972 decision to increase the primary school basic equipment grant was overdue. The long-established practice of subsidizing, dollar for dollar, money raised by school committees and parents' organizations for extra amenities has worked well in many communities but has failed in suburbs with a preponderance of low income families. Similarly, it is unrealistic in areas of special need to expect parents to raise money towards setting up pre-school centres. It is to be hoped, therefore, that a government decision announced early in 1970, to attach 'experimentally' a pre-school classroom to a primary school in Porirua East, Wellington's biggest and fastest-growing state housing development, points to a general policy trend, greater government support for pre-schooling. Certainly, if the recommendations of the 1971 Committee of Inquiry into Pre-School Education are followed, and it is likely they will be, government involvement, already financially considerable, will be much greater. At present, pre-school services are provided by two state-subsidized voluntary agencies, the Free Kindergarten Union and the Play Centre Federation. A departmental officer for Pre-School Education and twelve Pre-School Advisers provide pro-fessional advice. Kindergartens and play centres, however, cater for only a third of the population aged between three and five and they are seldom found where they are needed most, that is in new, high density housing areas and in country districts. The accuracy of the assertion that 'there are few other countries in the world known to the Department with a higher proportion than this' (*A to J*, 1970, E–1, 10) is questionable. The Committee of Inquiry recommended 'that, in the interests of children, parents, and the community, pre-school services should be expanded until they are ultimately available to all who wish to use them' (Pre-School Committee of Inquiry,

1971, 100). In 1973 kindergarten teacher training was incorporated in two teachers' colleges and greatly increased subsidies for play centres were announced.

6

Education and the Maori

New Zealand is not unique in that its more educationally under-privileged children are in country districts and new housing areas. But such underprivilege is especially serious in New Zealand where nearly 50 per cent of the children of the indigenous Polynesian people, the Maoris—about whose education there has been much concern since the late 1950s—still attend country schools and many more are at school in the new suburbs of North Island cities.

Concern for the formal education of Maori children and youth is not new; it goes back to 1816 when Church of England missionaries established a school at Paihia in the Bay of Islands in the far north of New Zealand. But it has been heightened in the period since 1945 by striking changes in the size and distribution of the Maori population, changes which are causing many New Zealanders, Maori and Pakeha, to speak of 'the Maori problem'. The most striking of these changes, the enforced migration of rural Maoris into urban centres in search of work, has revealed in the cities pockets of latent anti-Maori prejudice, the existence of which calls into question the validity of New Zealand's post-war claim to be a country in which there are two races but only one people.

Changing attitudes to the Maori

The attitude of white New Zealanders to their brown-skinned fellow-settlers has undergone a number of changes during the century which has elapsed since the end of the Pakeha–Maori Wars of the 1860s. For the first fifty years the Pakehas believed that the Maoris were, as a clergyman remarked in 1907, 'a people sick unto death'. The Maoris themselves despaired of the future. 'The white man looks on the men, the trees and the birds and they wither and die. I and my people are like dead trees in a forest clearing. One falls and another falls and soon we shall all be gone' (Baucke, 1928, 131). At the turn of the century, Apirana Ngata, Maori leader, politician and scholar, wrote of his people as 'battling bravely, nobly against the fates . . . braced with the hope that the day may yet be won . . . yet gladly dying with the knowledge that though their race is lost, it had died hard, bravely and nobly' (Ngata, 1893, 9). Under such circumstances all that the Pakeha needed to do was, as one of them unctuously remarked, 'smooth the pillow of a dying race'.

Education was seen as making easier the passing of the Maoris and facilitating the speedy absorption of any survivors into the general population. In 1867, to augment the work of the state-aided Anglican, Wesleyan and Catholic mission schools, the New Zealand parliament passed the first colonial education act, the Native Schools Act. Free secular village schools were established for 'children of the aboriginal native race and half-castes being orphans or the children of indigent parents', under the control of the Department of Native Affairs. Twelve years later these 'village schools' had become so numerous that they were transferred to the Maori School Service, a special branch of the newly formed Department of Education.

For in spite of predictions the Maori race declined to die; rather, from the beginning of this century, its numbers increased quite sharply. This unexpected resurgence occasioned instances of overt racial hostility by hitherto tolerant Pakehas. So long, however, as the Maoris stayed in remote or isolated country districts, little real conflict between the races was to be feared. Deliberate separation of the races was never attempted by any government nor, one would hope, considered, but a number of the economic, social and educational measures adopted by the government in the early 1930s (beginning with the Land and Development Act of 1929) had something of this effect. During the depression between 1930 and 1935 race relations in New Zealand reached a very low ebb when thousands of Maoris were reduced to a bare subsistence level. Employers discriminated against Maori workers in favour of jobless Pakehas; less Public Works relief was made available to Maoris because, it was said, they could always catch a few eels in a creek if they were hungry. The depression years made it quite clear that many Pakehas thought of Maoris as second-class citizens of limited intelligence. The apparent failure of all but a handful of Maoris to benefit from the educational opportunities available to them confirmed this belief. The Maori's place, it was generally agreed, was on the land;

only the educated few should be encouraged to go to the cities. The school's task, a Director of Education, T. B. Strong said, was to teach, 'the Maori lad to be a good farmer, and the girl to be a good farmer's wife' (Jackson, 1931, 192).

This stress in Maori education persisted throughout the 1930s although there were already clear signs that before very long there would not be enough land to support the now rapidly-growing Maori population. The 1936 census, for example, showed that almost half New Zealand's 82,000 Maoris were under twenty-one.

The Department of Education responded by giving the curriculum of Maori schools a manual–technical bias in place of its former agricultural one. The new emphasis was particularly evident in the Native District High Schools, the first of which was opened in 1941 by the Labour Government in a bid to fulfil its 1939 under-taking to provide secondary education for every child 'of the kind for which he is best fitted and to the fullest extent of his powers'. In these Native District High Schools the curriculum core was officially termed 'homemaking'. The boys were to be taught the elements of carpentry, and its associated trades with 'the definite aim of preparing them for the building trade' (*A to J*, 1941, E–1, 5) while the girls were to learn cooking, sewing and general house-wifery. Instruction in agriculture was not dropped altogether because it was widely, if naively, believed in the 1930s and early 1940s that such courses, by 'according status and dignity to the work of the farmer', helped to check any undue movement of population towards the towns (*NZ Education Gazette*, 1 May 1943, 91).

The new manual–technical curriculum of the Native District High Schools (Maori was not substituted for Native until 1948) was more than an educational innovation. It also reflected an official awareness that young Maoris, who could not longer be sure of employment on the land, and left the communal security of their tribal districts and townships to seek work in the predominantly Pakeha towns and cities, should be adequately prepared. As it was generally agreed that they had little aptitude for book-learning (McQueen, 1945), a notion apparently supported by the fact that up to 1945 only thirty-five Maoris had earned university degrees, then it followed that they must be taught appropriate manual skills. The inculcation of these was duly stressed in most state secondary schools with large numbers of Maori pupils. However, many teachers were impressed by the national examination successes of pupils from the highly academic denominational Maori secondary schools, and encouraged their more able Maori pupils to prepare for the new School Certificate Examination, one of the options in which was Maori.

The decision to make Maori an examination subject has proved to be more significant than the substitution of a manual–technical bias for an agricultural one. It indicated a major change in Maori education policy. Formerly the schools had been regarded as a principal means of Europeanizing the Maoris; now they were to attempt what seemed almost the opposite and aim 'at restoring to the Maori his pride of race, initiative and confidence' (*A to J*, 1944, E–1, 10). Peter Fraser, the Prime Minister from early 1940, Minister of Maori Affairs after 1946 and, until 1940, Minister of Education, was determined that Maoris should enter the mainstream of the country's social and economic life without any sense of inferiority and, as nearly as possible, on equal terms with the Pakehas.

Ironically, although Fraser strongly disliked criticism, however well intentioned, of Maoris, it was in 1941, very soon after he had relinquished the portfolio of Education, that a group of teachers in Waiapu County, a predominantly Maori district north of Gisborne, circulated among branches of the New Zealand Educational Institute a document which soon became highly contentious.

Entitled *The East Coast Maori Today*, the Waiapu report covered all aspects of Maori life on the isolated East Coast of the North Island, describing in considerable detail what its authors clearly regarded as a lamentable state of affairs. A somewhat emotional analysis of local conditions was followed by a number of excellent and practical recommendations for educational, social and economic reform. The value and sense of these were ignored in the political furore which greeted the Waiapu revelations. Maori leaders took the strongest possible exception to the report's contents; the mood of the East Coast Maoris became increasingly ugly; there was even fear in Wellington that should enemy troops land along the East Coast they would find support among the local inhabitants. At Fraser's insistence the Institute suppressed the report and apologized unreservedly for what was tactfully described as an error of judgment on the Institute's part for allowing such an overstated document to be circulated. Although the Institute executive knew there was much in the Waiapu report that was true, it was not prepared to meddle further in such a politically sensitive area (Ramsay, 1969).

Having burnt its fingers once, the Institute was not to be caught again. For the next twenty years Institute executives side-stepped, with varying degrees of adroitness, requests made to it by member branches for inquiries into the state of Maori education. The Institute's caution was understandable. After a burst of legislative activity between 1936 and 1945 had brought the Maori to equality with the Pakeha under the law, leaving on the Statute Books only such discriminatory legislation as was deemed to favour the Maori, it had become almost heresy to suggest that race relations in New Zealand were anything less than perfect.

There was a certain ostrich-like quality about this officially endorsed piece of folk-lore because, while it was true that, after 1935, the feelings and attitudes of the Pakeha towards the Maori mellowed, in fact a degree of racial prejudice and discrimination continued— and continues—to exist. State ways cannot change folk ways over-night. Peter Fraser's sharp reaction to the Waiapu report and his similar reaction a few years later to a clergyman's use of extracts from the report in a broadcast church service, suggest that he sensed a certain brittleness in race relations in New Zealand. The ambivalence of the Pakeha's attitude towards the Maori was pinpointed by a visiting American scholar who said that he had met many Pakehas who, after boasting of the lack of a colour-bar in New Zealand, then gave vent to quite savage anti-Maori feelings (Ausubel, 1960). Many New Zealanders were secretly aware of this latent prejudice and were ashamed of it. What few realized was that the movement of the Maori away from the land, especially for war work, had precipitated the clash of cultures inevitable in all modern multi-racial societies. The consequent friction was intensified by the limited range of educational and work skills possessed by the migratory ethnic group.

Facing facts

Statistically in the post-war census returns, visibly in the streets of the cities, the growing proportion of Maoris in the total population became apparent. The numbers of Maori children attending North Island city schools soared, especially in Auckland, rapidly becoming what it now is, the largest Polynesian city in the world. More and more labourers on building projects, men engaged in the perennial New Zealand pastime of digging up the city streets, unskilled workers everywhere, tended to be Maoris. Magistrates commented on the high proportion of young Maori offenders who came before them and secondary school teachers in urban schools noted an increasing preponderance of brown-skinned children in the lower streams of first and second year classes. All these signs, the potential dire significance of which was highlighted in 1958 by Professor Ausubel, led to a growing unease among a large section of the public about the position, present and future, of the Maori in the community.

The problem was clearly complex and needed to be attacked on many fronts. Accordingly, the Department of Maori Affairs prepared a report published in 1960 (usually referred to as the Hunn Report after the then Secretary for Maori Affairs) which attempted to look squarely at all aspects of what was glibly termed 'the Maori problem'. The report's authors surveyed the fields of education, employment, crime, health, housing and welfare as statistically and objectively as they could and came to the unpalatable conclusion that, whatever New Zealanders might wish to believe, the Maoris were indeed a depressed ethnic minority whose members, as things were, had little chance of improving their position.

The section of the report on education stressed that, although public schooling was the same for Pakeha and Maori alike, the latter seemed not to have derived as great a benefit from it. Small numbers of young Maoris stayed on at secondary school to enter the sixth forms and an even smaller number went on to university. Possible reasons for Maori children's comparative lack of academic success were not spelled out but the report made one especially valuable suggestion. It recommended the establishment of a Maori Education Foundation, whose endowment income could be used, in particular, to assist Maori students in secondary schools and tertiary institutions (Hunn, 1960). This suggestion was accepted by the government; in November 1961, the Maori Education Foundation Act provided for an initial government grant of £125,000 and a pound for pound subsidy on voluntary contributions.

In a foreword to the Hunn Report the Minister of Maori Affairs wrote that, although some of the issues were controversial, he did not think they should be suppressed. Certainly the report gave rise to a spate of inquiries about the place of the Maori in the New Zealand community. It was as if a perplexing, private anxiety of many organizations could for the first time be discussed openly with complete frankness. The New Zealand Post-Primary Teachers' Association (1961), the Commission on Education (1962), the Department of Labour and Employment (1964) and the Opotiki Branch of the New Zealand Educational Institute (1964) were the first to conduct their own inquiries and make public their findings. More recently, the Department of Industries and Commerce (1967), the New Zealand Educational Institute (1967) and the National Development Conference (1968) have followed suit. Because the Hunn Report seems to have expunged memories of the Waiapu incident twenty years before, these reports of the 1960s are frank and forthright in their analyses of the problems facing the Maoris in modern New Zealand society, and constructive in their approach to the question of how young Maoris can improve their qualifications.

However, in the past two decades, the most immediately practical suggestions for improving Maori education have come, appropriately, from a special advisory committee, the National Committee on Maori Education, convened in 1955 by the Minister of Education at the request of his department which had concluded that its separate Maori School Service was no longer necessary, and that in their own best interests all Maori children should attend, as two-thirds of them already did, ordinary education board primary schools. But some rural Maoris looked upon their separate schools almost as an extension of the *marae*, the centre of community life, and the department hesitated to take the initiative and close them. A further complication was that the land on which some Maori Service schools were built had been gifted by the local people. In such a community an education board school would be, as one Maori writer put it, 'like a pearl in an oyster, highly valued but not entirely part of it'. Opposition was also expected from teachers in the service who for a number of reasons, including the fact that a more favourable staff to pupil ratio was allowed in Maori schools, believed that it was still in the best interests of the Maori to retain the existing arrangements. A former Senior Inspector of Maori Schools foresaw nothing but ill in the proposed abolition of the Maori Service. 'I think', he wrote, 'the wisest course might be to leave well alone in the meantime, and not spoil a very good system of Maori education' (*Dominion*, 14 September 1955).

But the National Committee on Maori Education (on which the Maoris, for the first time at the national level were well represented), did not agree. Its members were as concerned as senior departmental officers at the slow scholastic progress of Maori children in primary schools and were prepared to try new measures. They agreed that the transference of Maori Service schools to education board control would, in the long run, be desirable, although they did not want the process unduly rushed. 'When it is decided by the Director of Education that a school is ready for transfer . . .,' the Committee resolved, 'full consultation must first be held with the local Maori people.'

Transfers began in 1956 and continued slowly and somewhat spasmodically for a decade. Then in 1966 the National Committee on Maori Education, which has met annually since 1955 to review policy and practice and co-ordinate action on the part of various interested groups, recommended that at a fixed date not before February 1969, all Maori schools should be transferred to board control, a measure subsequently made effective as from that date.

Acted on with greater speed was the recommendation that school committees of Maori schools which had very restricted powers 'be placed on the same basis as the schools committees of board schools in all respects'. This was suggested, partly to involve Maori parents more closely with the work of the schools, and partly to prepare them to take their place later with Pakeha parents on board school committees. Some headteachers opposed the proposal but the Department of Education welcomed it. The Education Amendment Act of 1957 gave the committees of Maori schools all the powers and responsibilities, such as they are, enjoyed by the committees of education board schools. The Director of Education, in his annual report, commented, it might be thought patronizingly, that the new status of the committees gave 'further recognition of the ability of the Maori people to shoulder the full responsibilities of New Zealand citizens' (*A to J*, 1958, E–1, 44).

Another administrative recommendation made by the National Committee on Maori Education in 1955 was accepted even more promptly by the department. The Senior Inspector of Maori Schools had his position upgraded to that of Officer for Maori

Education and was made responsible for the educational and general welfare of Maori pupils in board as well as Maori schools. Within months the first Officer for Maori Education stimulated interest and concern about Maori education to such an extent that his director could write of the heightened awareness among education board members and officials, and among inspectors and teachers, of the special problems of Maori children in certain areas (*A to J*, 1956, E–1, 33).

The committee's list of suggestions to improve Maori education was extremely wide ranging. A direct result was that teachers' colleges began to develop, some more successfully and fully than others, courses related to Maori education and culture so that future teachers would understand better the difficulties faced by Maori school children. As a minority group among Pakehas, Maori children need to develop a sense of security, personal worth and identity. The committee therefore proposed that greater emphasis should be given in primary schools to the teaching of Maori history, legends, songs, art and crafts. This emphasis, it was hoped, would also make the Pakeha child more aware and appreciative of the distinctive contribution made by the Maori people to New Zealand life.

Plenty of opportunity had been afforded to discuss and teach things Maori in the primary school social studies syllabus after its revision in 1948, but teachers and pupils were handicapped by the lack of suitable literature. This deficiency was largely overcome, after the National Committee on Maori Education had pointed it out in 1955, through the combined efforts of the School Publications and the Art and Crafts branches of the department in preparing a specialized series of bulletins and manuals 'designed to strengthen Maori culture'.

Curriculum and administration matters have concerned the National Committee on Maori Education most since 1955; it has constantly asked: 'How can this or that feature of the school system be changed or adapted to increase the interest of Maori children and their parents in education?' On the other hand, the Commission on Education, with different terms of reference asked: 'Why is it that, in spite of special provision for Maori education through the Maori School Service and a complete lack of discrimination between Maori and Pakeha pupils in schools under education and secondary school boards, the educational attainment of the typical Maori youngster is usually inferior to that of the Pakeha youngster? Why is it that a much greater proportion of Maori pupils than Pakeha leave school at fifteen; that whereas 29·7 per cent of Pakeha pupils attain School Certificate or better, only 4·8 per cent of Maori pupils reach this level; that at the university stage the number of Maori students enrolled, to be proportionate to the number of Pakeha students, would need raising by a factor of eight?' (Commission on Education, 1962, 402–8).

Some reasons for this state of affairs were apparent; others were not. The commission's recommendations were designed, therefore, to tidy up existing confusions and to provide a blueprint for future development. It urged appropriate agencies to undertake more research into social, linguistic and pedagogical aspects of Maori education. Although this advice was followed, it was still possible for the Assistant-Director of the New Zealand Council for Educational Research to remark five years later that 'the data that would be required for a discerning assessment of the scholastic achievement of Maori children have not yet been assembled' (Watson, 1967, 21). Nevertheless, present understanding of the causes of Maori educational under-achievement is unquestionably greater than it was in 1960 when the Department of Maori Affairs publicly examined its own stewardship and the Commission on Education decided to go beyond its specific terms of reference and to make the education of the Maori the subject of a special inquiry.

Social causes of under-achievement

Socio-economic conditions are a major factor in denying Maori children equality of educational opportunity. The Hunn Report threw into relief the wide social and economic gap existing in 1960 between Maori and Pakeha, and the censuses of 1961 and 1966 revealed that this gap was not closing as quickly as might be hoped. The 1966 census, for example, showed that nearly 90 per cent of Maori men were unskilled or semi-skilled and that only 5 per cent of them, compared with 32 per cent of Pakehas, were employed in urban white-collar jobs. The female distribution was similarly skewed towards unskilled and semi-skilled work. The unskilled or seasonal nature of much of their work was reflected in the incomes of the Maori wage-earners. 'In 1966', the Government Statistician pointed out, 'only eight per cent of Maoris with incomes had more than $2,599 compared with 21·3 per cent for the total population' (*Evening Post*, 28 May 1969).

In spite of this clear-cut statistical evidence, few New Zealand educationists will accept that social class and home background are the only causes of the low achievement of so many Maori students. They agree, however, that social status is significant as long as children's educational aspirations are directly influenced by their own and parental assessments of the school's relevance to employment prospects. Since the importance of an extended education is seldom appreciated by parents with limited occupational horizons, the typical Maori child is unlikely to be encouraged to do well at school in the way Pakeha parents encourage their children. 'Pakeha parents demand higher school marks than Maori parents and prod more about homework' (Ausubel, 1961, 162).

This is not to say that Maori parents do not value education; many of them simply fail to realize that for the school to be effective they, too, have a part to play. And other parents who do understand the importance of the environment in educational success, may still be unable to do much to create the desired home background because the typical Maori family, in town or country, lives under more crowded conditions than a Pakeha family. The 1961 census returns showed that the average Maori married man had 3·64 children to support, compared with the Pakeha's 2·10 children. Further, Maoris living in the towns often have country relatives who are looking for work staying with them for lengthy periods. Faulty nutrition and ill-health, a Department of Health report showed in 1960, are associated hazards. The Commission on Education report summed up the position in one sentence. 'Too many [Maori children]', it said, 'live in large families in inadequately sized and even primitive houses, lacking privacy, quiet, and even light for study: too often there is a dearth of books, pictures, educative material generally, to stimulate the growing child' (Commission on Education, 1962, 418). One research student remarked that in many of the homes she visited the principal reading matter available consisted of the Bible, *Best Bets* and comics (Smith, 1958).

In addition to these obvious social handicaps, a Maori child may be held back by intransigent cultural factors such as his or her relations with parents. In young and growing Maori families the younger children get most parental attention; one or two of the older children may be sent to live with grandparents but in any case will certainly be left to fend for themselves. As children grow up, there may be little communication between parents and adolescents and few chances to discuss school problems and vocational future (Ritchie, 1963, 103–19).

A very real problem for all research workers is to distinguish between handicaps in school which are attributable to social class, and handicaps which are a reflection of the particular Maori values or residuals in a child's heritage (Watson, 1967, 10). Until such distinctions can be made it will be difficult to mount a successful multi-pronged attack on the problem of Maori educational under-achievement which is urgently needed. A Maori research programme initiated by the New Zealand Council for Educational Research in 1971, with government financial support may give some direction.

Language difficulties

In the past few years the language difficulties of Maori children have attracted particular attention. Maori school children, just entering school as five- or six-year-olds from homes where an indifferent mixture of English and Maori is spoken, have weaknesses in verbal fluency which in many cases they never overcome and which adversely affect their whole school career. Certainly, many Pakeha children also begin school with language deficiencies, but their chance of help from home is better than for most Maori children. The Welfare Controller for the Department of Maori and Island Affairs ascribes the educational backwardness of so many Maori children to 'verbal paralysis', an inability to communicate in English and to grasp what the teacher is saying. With this judgment most teachers of Maori children agree, although they cannot determine precisely the nature of these language difficulties. One study on the English vocabulary and sentence structure of Maori children suggested that lack of vocabulary was the chief impediment to their educational progress. The author found that the English vocabulary of tested Maori children was sometimes as much as two years behind that of Pakeha children from approximately the same socio-economic background (Barham, 1965).

So far as the language of instruction is concerned, Maori children receive no concessions when they enter school. Even though linguists have, on a number of occasions, recommended a bilingual approach in primary schools with large Maori enrolments, Maori, admitted as a subject for the B.A. degree in 1925, for University Entrance, first from 1923 to 1948 and then continuously from 1950, and for School Certificate in 1945, was not, until 1971, included in the primary school curriculum. Indeed, it is said that in the 1930s, corporal punishment was meted out to children overheard speaking Maori in the playground. Rather curiously, efforts to eradicate the Maori language in schools were almost unopposed by Maori leaders. They seem to have agreed with Sir Apirana Ngata, their doyen, that English should be 'first, second and third in the school curriculum' (*Gisborne Herald*, 2 December 1940). They believed that Maori could be preserved through its use in the home and on the *marae*; that its preservation was no concern of the schools; that only by mastering English could the Maori hope to hold his own in a competitive Pakeha society. The result was that before long the majority of younger Maoris could neither speak nor understand their mother tongue so when the Department of Education agreed, at the request of the National Committee on Maori Education in 1955, to assist in the teaching of Maori, the language was commonly spoken only by older people. It still remained the primary language in a small number of rural districts but even there its continued existence was threatened by the transistor radio and the impending introduction of television.

Largely as a result of the National Committee's recommendation, the department set up a committee on the teaching of the Maori language to assist in preparing language texts for secondary schools and to advise, among other things, on the correct form of the language.

The current difficulty, that there are few qualified teachers of Maori, may disappear in the 1970s. Early in 1973 the government approved the appointment of lecturers in Maori language in primary teachers' colleges. Yet while in recent years the number of people formally studying Maori at school, teachers' colleges, university or through university extension courses, has increased sharply, Maori is rarely spoken in the streets. There are few opportunities to read or speak the language. No newspaper publishes a column in Maori; the New Zealand Broadcasting Corporation offers only a short weekly radio newscast in Maori. And apart from the quarterly, *Te Ao Hou* (The New World), published by the Department of Maori and Island Affairs on behalf of the Maori Purposes Trust Board, hardly any magazine or journal has a substantial Maori content.

Attempts to overcome the handicaps

The remarkable range of inquiries conducted in the 1960s into the causes of low educational achievement among Maori youngsters, was matched by the variety of attempts made by the Department of Education to overcome the revealed handicaps. It encouraged the establishment of homework centres to alleviate the problem of overcrowding in Maori homes. After 1965 it allowed schools with large Maori enrolments to employ part-time teachers to provide additional reading instruction; it approved the appointment of the first adviser on language for Maori children; and encouraged the teachers' colleges (although not until 1973 as whole-heartedly as some staff members would have liked), to extend and enlarge their Polynesian Studies courses. Departmental officers, either directly or indirectly provided in-service training courses in the teaching of English as a second language, the educational consequences of social deprivation, and the special needs of Maori and Pacific Island pupils. *Maori Children and the Teacher*, a departmental handbook intended to help teachers to assess the background of their Polynesian pupils, was published in 1971. In addition, the department consistently gives its blessing and active support where this is needed, to the development of a pre-school service for Maori children, recognizing, with the New Zealand Educational Institute, that the pre-school experiences of the Maori child 'indelibly mark his path through life' (*NZEI*, 1968, 39).

The department also awards 140 scholarships annually to country children who have at least 50 per cent Polynesian blood to enable them to travel to, or board at, private or state secondary schools which offer courses not available locally (*NZ Education Gazette*, 16 March 1970, 106).

The work of the Maori Education Foundation

When the Maori Education Foundation was first established the chairman of its board of trustees, a former Senior Inspector of

Maori Schools, said that the foundation's main function would be the creation of an educated élite. This notion did not find favour everywhere. There was no guarantee, the critics said, that an educated minority would fulfil the leadership role the foundation chairman envisaged. 'This is a pseudo-argument,' a former Pakeha editor of *Te Ao Hou* wrote. 'Elites in other developing populations have often tended to form a social class of their own, aloof from the mass. This is already happening in the Maori élite' (Schwimmer, 1962, 9).

As a direct outcome, the aims of the foundation were broadened. The stress on helping a young Maori élite was muted somewhat and more emphasis placed on creating greater awareness among New Zealanders of the Maori's educational plight while at the same time encouraging Maori parents to support the education of their children. Most significantly, the foundation turned its attention to pre-school education. 'Our major objective is clear,' the chairman told his board of trustees; 'to strengthen Maori home life and the language, general knowledge and experience of children in their crucial pre-school years until every Maori child is as well equipped as the European child to come to school' (*Evening Post*, 22 August 1962).

Pre-school education

By the 1960s enough was known about child-rearing practices in Maori families to indicate that the Maori youngster entering school would not respond to this new environment like his Pakeha classmates. The difference in language ability was usually apparent. Not so apparent, but possibly of much greater significance, was the fact that, unless he came from a highly acculturated home, the personality of the Maori five-year-old was fundamentally different from that of his Pakeha classmates. The typical Maori five-year-old entered school with attitudes of self-depreciation acquired from his parents and family. As a result he was often immobilized by *whakama* (a Maori term meaning embarrassment, shyness and alienation), whenever he found himself in a strange situation (Watson, 1967, 27). These feelings, so intense that few Maori children can talk about them, may impede educational progress throughout their school lives.

To reduce this shock and to give greater confidence and competence in the use of English the foundation, in its second year of life (1963), appointed a Pre-School Officer to assist Maori parents to establish pre-school centres and to encourage them to take a greater interest in the growth and development, intellectual as well as physical, of their children.

Maori parents responded enthusiastically to the visits of the Pre-School Officer and, by 1968, 472 centres for children had been set up, mainly in the rural areas of the northern half of the North Island. In addition, courses were offered which aimed 'to develop in parents the art of observing their own children . . ., and to notice ways of helping [them] enjoy learning' (Maori Education Foundation, 1965, 12). Such enthusiasm was aroused that in many districts in the Waikato where it was not possible to establish play centres, Maori mothers themselves organized informal family play groups in private houses. In 1968 the Foundation undertook to do what it could to help these groups. To all of them the foundation makes available copies of its film on child development, *As the Twig is Bent*, and the accompanying book, *Tamariki*, both prepared in 1965.

In its enthusiasm for pre-school education the foundation did not lose sight of its original objective, the fostering of education at senior secondary and tertiary levels. Financial help is generously given and foundation-appointed part-time liaison officers in the universities keep in touch with Maori students. Many Maori students are also eligible to receive money from sources other than the foundation or the Department of Education. For example, a number of trusts are financed by the Maoris themselves. The Tuwharetoa tribe, a wealthy tribe whose extensive lands were not confiscated after the Pakeha–Maori Wars, is one which makes grants to its student members from the fifth form upwards.

The Maori in the work force

Maori migrants to the urban centres, however, continue to contribute raw labour rather than skill to the work force. While 30 per cent of all New Zealand male school leavers took up apprenticeships in the 1960s, fewer than 10 per cent of Maori boys did so. The reasons for this are not hard to find. First, many Maori boys leave school before they have reached the educational standard required for acceptance as an apprentice. Second, in some country settlements it is hard for a school leaver to find a job of any sort and practically impossible to learn a skilled trade. Third, many private employers prefer to engage young Pakehas with little education rather than Maoris with little education (Vellekoop, 1968). Perhaps inevitably, Maori parents seem to accept more readily than Pakehas the notion that their sons will have to take up manual work. One survey, for example, of parental attitudes showed that 56 per cent of Maori parents compared with 29 per cent of Pakehas were resigned to their sons becoming un-skilled workers.

The Department of Maori and Island Affairs, a government agency set up as the Department of Native Affairs in 1852 (the name was changed to Maori Affairs in 1939), and now owing its continued existence largely to the need for specialized knowledge of the intricacies of Maori land ownership, established in 1959, on an experimental basis, in conjunction with the technical college in Auckland, a pre-apprenticeship scheme designed to widen the spread of occupational skills among young Maoris moving into the towns. The number and variety of courses grew, within eight years, from a single trade offered in one technical institute, to seven trades in three institutes, and from an initial intake of ten to one of 156 boys. Entry to these courses has become highly competitive; only half of those who apply are accepted. The minimum entry qualification is two years of secondary schooling. All but one of the courses are for one year; the carpentry course, because of the practical work involved, is spread over two years. All trainees receive special coaching in English and mathematics so that when they embark on their apprenticeships they will be able to handle satisfactorily what-ever theoretical work is involved.

Limited facilities and accommodation and the high cost per trainee have prevented the rapid increase of these pre-apprenticeship courses. Nevertheless they indicate what can be done to tap New Zealand's greatest reservoir of unused talent. A rise in the percentage of Maoris among apprentices from 2·4 to 5·4 per cent in nine years (*Evening Post*, 25 November 1969) is some measure of how Maori youths can be prevented from gravitating towards unskilled work. The outstanding later successes of boys who took these courses should encourage private employers to recruit and train rural Maoris for skilled work in industry.

The Department of Maori and Island Affairs (which co-operates with the Department of Education through an inter-departmental committee) also helps young Maoris from the country to deal with the complexities of city life by means of pre-employment, 'Live in a City', courses offered, first in Wellington in 1966 and then later in Auckland, in association with the local technical institutes. At these, Maori boys and girls seeking jobs follow a five-week programme of lectures, discussions and visits after which the department helps them to find permanent employment. Hostels, usually run by churches aided by the government, give newcomers a chance to get used to urban living. The Vocational Guidance Service, established in 1938 by the Departments of Education and Labour but re-organized in 1943 and integrated with the Department of Education, does a good deal for young Maoris recently arrived in the cities. Its effectiveness was, however, reduced in the 1960s because of difficulties in recruiting and retaining staff.

The task ahead

Since 1945 much has been done to help the Maoris take advantage of available educational opportunities. Above all, difficulties facing Maori boys and girls are better understood and attempts are being made to improve communication between schools and Maori and Polynesian parents. It is realized that unless positive and effective measures to improve the educational performance of Maori youngsters are maintained and extended, situations could arise in New Zealand that would give race relations a cutting edge they have not had for a century. An unpleasant indicator was the three to one difference in Maori and Pakeha unemployment rates during the 1967-8 recession. The social implications of such a situation during a more serious depression are obvious. New Zealand governments, and the Pakeha majority in general, cannot afford to overlook or ignore the peculiar educational needs and circumstances of an ethnic minority of 200,000 (now 8 per cent of the country's total population) when half that minority is under the age of fifteen, its birth-rate is twice that of the Pakeha majority, and its crude death-rate is very little higher.

Educationally the prospects for advance are considerably better in the 1970s than they were a decade earlier. While the Maori

Education Foundation failed to 'transform education in ten years', as predicted in the Hunn Report, it made appreciable progress, given the magnitude of its task and its limited resources. In 1966 there were, for example, more Maori students at Auckland University than there had been at all the New Zealand universities in 1956; 9 per cent of all secondary school pupils were Maori in 1969 compared with 8 per cent in 1964; there was a 40·5 per cent increase in the numbers of Maori fifth and sixth formers between 1966–8. Maori pupils were staying longer at school and leaving it better qualified. In 1965, 1·96 per cent of Maori school leavers had a University Entrance qualification or better, 2·74 per cent had Endorsed School Certificate and 9·79 per cent had School Certificate. By 1968 these percentages had risen to 2·62, 4·64 and 13·71 respectively. These are hopeful signs for which the foundation can take a large share of the credit.

TABLE 2   Increase in primary and secondary school enrolments, 1962–72

	1962	1972	% increase
All primary enrolment	440,163	518,904	17·9
Maori primary enrolment	50,359	73,527	46·0
All secondary enrolment	141,318	196,655	39.2
Maori secondary enrolment	9,432	19,584	107·6
All schools enrolment	581,481	715,559	23·1
Maori pupils	79,791	93,107	16·7

(*Source*: R. Mahuta: University of Waikato)

However, the public, Pakeha and Maori alike, need to be aware that such cheering official statistics were affected by increases in Maori enrolments and by outside influences such as the recession which temporarily encouraged many young New Zealanders to stay at school. There is no room for complacency; Maori students at all levels still have a long way to go to match the performance of Pakeha children. While perhaps the greatest challenge facing New Zealanders today is that presented by the task of equipping the rising generation of young Maoris to take its full part in national life, success in meeting this challenge will only be possible if the Maori people themselves take greater responsibility for furthering the education of their youth. They must encourage them, as Sir Apirana Ngata did an earlier generation, not only to cherish Maori culture but also to master the arts of the Pakeha. 'Turn your hand to the tools of the Pakeha for the well-being of your body,' Ngata wrote in a child's autograph book, 'turn your heart to the treasures of your ancestors as a crown for your head.'

New Zealand and her Polynesian neighbours

Because of New Zealand's geography and history and the dual racial origin of her people, successive governments have accepted particular responsibility, although at times reluctantly, for educational developments in New Zealand's 'near north'. Educational aid has been given not only to those islands of Polynesia with whose administration New Zealand has been directly concerned—Niue, the Cook Islands, Western Samoa and the Tokelaus—but also to Fiji, Tonga, the Gilbert and Ellice Islands and Pitcairn Island.

In 1945 a resurgence of nationalism in Western Samoa and United Nations' proposals for new trusteeship schemes for territories held under mandate from the League of Nations roused the New Zealand Government to a new sense of its responsibilities, economic, political and educational, in the islands. An Islands Education Office was established as a division of the Department of Education in Wellington to stimulate and guide educational development. The pre-war fear that too much education 'would upset the equilibrium of the islands' (Ross, ed., 1969, 284) gave way in the post-war period to a realization that if the increasing numbers of islanders who were migrating to New Zealand were not to become an economically and socially depressed minority, then the quality of the education they received in their home islands would have to be improved.

To help in raising educational standards, increased numbers of New Zealand teachers were recruited for service in the islands; more islands students were awarded scholarships to enable them to attend New Zealand schools, teachers' colleges and universities; provision was made for the extension of teacher training facilities in Western Samoa and the Cook Islands and, in the 1950s, a secondary school was established in both territories. The failure of the New Zealand administration to develop secondary education earlier, and its unwillingness to make more than limited provision when it did, retarded political and economic progress in Western Samoa and the Cook Islands and, it is alleged, made the inhabitants less ready than they might have been for their independence in the 1960s.

Although the New Zealand Department of Education now has little direct responsibility for schooling in the South Pacific, it continues to contribute to educational development in the region not only by recruiting teachers in New Zealand for service in island schools and maintaining an inspection service for them, but by supervising sponsored students and in-service trainees, by preparing specialized textbooks, especially in the teaching of English as a second language, and by providing teaching aids and library books to certain school systems.

TABLE 3   Changes in Maori population, 1857–1971

Census	Maori population	% of total population	Average annual increase in previous 5 years
1857–8	56,049	48·6	—
1874	47,330	13·7	—
1881	46,141	8·6	—
1896	42,113	5·7	—
1901	45,549	5·6	1·6
1921	56,987	4·5	1·6
1926	63,670	4·5	2·2
1936	82,326	5·2	2·6
1945	98,774	5·8	1·9
1951	115,676	6·0	2·9
1956	137,151	6·3	3·5
1961	167,086	6·9	4·0
1966	201,159	7·5	3·8
1971	227,414	8·0	2·5

PART THREE

Educational problems

7

Difficulties of implementing policy

With the return of peace in 1945 the Department of Education prepared to give practical expression to the government's pre-war promises of educational reform. Confident of government co-operation, and reasonably assured of public support, the department made ready to convert the school system, originally constructed on a basis of selection and privilege, to a more truly democratic form which would 'cater for the whole population' (*A to J*, 1939, E–1, 3). It promised a vigorous building programme to overcome the shortage of places which had developed during the war; better school accommodation, especially at secondary level, to allow for the full implementation of the newly-introduced secondary school curriculum designed to give every child 'a broad cultural education'; smaller classes; better-trained teachers; and some system of guidance in secondary schools to help the pupils select the courses most suitable for their abilities (*NZ Education Gazette*, 1 September 1946, 229).

But while planning for the future, the Director of Education, C. E. Beeby, warned that his department would have to take account of the existing problems posed by big classes and overcrowded schools.

The population explosion

The educational planners anticipated a sharp post-war increase in the school population—raising the school-leaving age to fifteen in 1945 alone made this inevitable—but were not prepared for the magnitude and persistence of the increase which actually occurred. It was so great that it probably limited educational reform more significantly than any other factor. Primary school enrolments, which had remained static at about 280,000 from 1930–43 had, by 1951, reached 351,000, and by 1955, 453,000. The annual average increase of 10,000 pupils each year from 1943–50 rose to 20,000

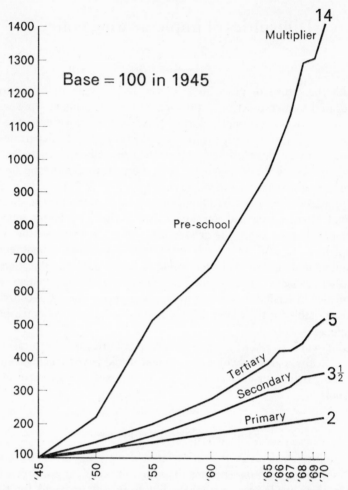

Figure 2   Booming rolls, 1945–70 (Source: Department of Education)

between 1950 and 1955, and in 1959 it remained as high as 18,000.

Birth-rate statistics for the period throw light on the troubles of the schools; in 1933 there were 27,000 births, in 1945, 39,000, in 1946, 50,000 and in 1955, 56,000. It was difficult for the educational planners to judge whether the immediate post-war increase in the birth-rate would be maintained. The general feeling in the Department of Education between 1946 and 1950 was that continuing substantial increases were not likely, that the problems of staffing and accommodation were only temporary, that the population bulge would move slowly through the school system and then disappear. But while this proved to be the case in England it was not so in New Zealand. Between 1945 and 1961 (when it began to decline) the birth-rate increased steadily from 24·6 to 27·0 per thousand. Because educational planning in New Zealand at this time was scarcely numerate, forecasting future enrolments became almost a matter of guesswork—and the guesses were not remarkably accurate. In 1950, for example, the departmental estimate of the secondary school population in 1959 was 66,000; there were, in fact, 90,000 pupils, an increase of 90 per cent, not 40 per cent, over the 1949 enrolment figure of 47,000 on which the prediction was based.

The accommodation crisis

Education boards, as the authorities immediately responsible for primary education, were presented with difficult problems of staffing and accommodation. Unable to speed up their building programmes, they were forced to turn to the Department of Education for help, reluctant though they were to lose any more of their already very limited autonomy. In response to the boards' requests, departmental architects, with the co-operation of the boards, evolved a standard type of primary school plan, the ingenious Dominion Basic Plan, which could be adapted easily to suit the wide variety of conditions and sites likely to be encountered in a country stretching a thousand miles from north to south. The general use of the Dominion Basic Plan between 1951 and 1955, when the demand for additional school buildings was at its peak, made it possible to accelerate the building of new schools or blocks of classrooms in spite of acute shortages of labour and building materials.

The need for increased speed and at the same time decreased costs, led the government, at the director's insistence, to send a departmental team to the United Kingdom in 1954 to study the planning and construction of schools there. On their return, the departmental officers tried to adapt English experience to New Zealand conditions. In the 1955 building code for primary schools they concentrated on avoiding waste space by incorporating part of the corridors, characteristic of so many New Zealand schools, in the actual classrooms. The extra space provided additional teaching space throughout the whole day while acting as circulation space on the relatively few occasions when children were moving from classroom to classroom. The total area per child was reduced from 33·1 square feet to 24·3 square feet. Higher standards were set for storage, administrative areas and staff accommodation.

At the same time, in an attempt to get full value for money spent on buildings and to put the onus on education board officers, the Department of Education introduced its so-called 'white-lines policy' under which the freedom to plan new school buildings within the two 'white lines' of minimum standards and maximum cost for each pupil–place was left to the education boards. Money saved could be spent by the boards on amenities of their choice. Education board administrators accepted the department's challenge, and until rising building costs made worthwhile economies difficult, the 'white lines policy' worked well.

There was, however, criticism of the close control exercised over school building by the department after the introduction of the Dominion Basic Plan. That the education boards co-operated as willingly as they did indicates the undoubted urgency of the situation, and the good personal relations which existed between the director and senior board officials by 1950. The development of standard plans for primary schools and the disappearance of features characteristic of the buildings of particular education boards was unavoidable if costs of school construction were not to become an intolerable burden on the economy.

Similarly, when a heavy secondary school building programme had to be started in 1953—between 1940 and 1953 not a single, completely new secondary school had been established—the development of standard plans by Department of Education and Ministry of Works architects was inevitable. Between 1945 and 1970 the number of secondary schools increased from 69 to 210. Secondary accommodation was so urgently needed in many areas that new schools were constructed in stages so that the first block could be occupied while work was proceeding on the next. School principals and their staffs are grimly resentful that this method of building schools has become endemic in New Zealand.

The teacher shortage

Given a few years and adequate finance the lack of accommodation could be overcome; the scarcity of teachers was a more complex and intractable problem and is still not completely solved in the secondary schools.

The causes of the teacher shortage in New Zealand are not difficult to determine. The high wartime enlistment rate among male teachers and teachers' college students was more than matched by the high percentage subsequently killed in action. And among many of those who returned, there was a marked reluctance to go back to the classroom. Few recruits entered the teaching profession by way of the teachers' colleges during the war years so some temporary shortages had to be expected. That these would soon be overcome was a vain hope because the size of the post-war population explosion was so under-estimated. But had the forecasts been approximately correct and the difficulties ahead more clearly seen, it is doubtful whether much could have been done to avert the primary school staffing crises of the 1950s. To cater for the 40,000 to 50,000 children born annually in the decade after 1945, student teachers had to be recruited from among young people born in the early 1930s when there had been only 27,000 births a year. Furthermore, teaching proved not to be as attractive after the war as before. By 1947 the possibility of a serious shortage of primary teachers was recognized and measures were taken to increase admission to the primary teacher training courses.

The minister drew attention to some rather obvious implications of the threatened understaffing. 'A greatly increased number of teachers', he predicted, 'will be necessary to enable the size of classes to be reduced and the period of teacher training to be extended by a year' (*A to J*, 1947, E–1, 7). His prediction proved distressingly accurate. For the next twenty years the emphasis was always upon the quantity, not the quality of the primary teachers available; the demand for numbers made worthwhile reforms in teacher education very difficult to bring about although, following the report of the Consultative Committee on Teacher Training in 1951, the teachers' colleges made determined efforts to raise standards of training. Their task was not made easier during these years when the entrance standards of college students reached their nadir. Unable to attract enough suitably qualified school leavers to take up the places available in the teachers' colleges, the Department of Education introduced in 1949 a one-year training scheme for suitable applicants over twenty-one. This special course, which over the years produced more than 2,400 teachers of very mixed quality, came to an end in 1960.

It was no coincidence that an officially designated emergency measure was discontinued then. Late in 1960 the director felt confident enough to assert that the worst of the primary teacher shortage was over. As a mark of this confidence he asked the government to bring into operation during 1961 and 1962 the more generous staffing schedules that had lain dormant in the regulations since 1948.

Although teacher supply prospects were better in 1960 than in 1950, there was still no room for complacency because of an annual 'wastage' rate of about 10 per cent among teachers in service. In 1961, senior primary service administrators in the Department of Education, were aware how easily the delicate staffing balance in the schools could be upset if too many young teachers left teaching soon after finishing their training and persuaded reluctant colleagues, and an even more reluctant New Zealand Educational Institute executive, to agree that, from 1962, as a condition of entry, all teachers' college students would have to contract to teach for the same number of years as their training or pay a substantial monetary penalty. This 'bond', as it is called, has never been popular in the teaching profession and there has been much agitation to have it done away with. The Institute, however, has always temporized on the issue so as not to jeopardize the promised introduction, between 1972 and 1976, of the improved 1:35 staffing schedules, a promise which, despite problems associated with the introduction of three-year teacher training, seems likely to be fulfilled.

At the end of the 1960s the staffing position in primary schools was reasonably satisfactory; in 1968, for example, the number of posts unfilled by regular teachers was down to 4·2 per cent—a substantial improvement on the 6 per cent at the beginning of the decade—and there were only twenty-two uncertificated teachers serving as relievers. With adequate numbers of better trained teachers entering the schools and the introduction of a new building code in 1970 incorporating the requirements of schools under the 1:35 staffing schedules, a bright future for the primary service seems assured. The high hopes of the immediate post-war years may yet be fulfilled.

The staffing position in the secondary schools in the early 1970s, on the other hand, gives less ground for similar optimism. Staff shortages have dogged the secondary schools for a quarter of a century. They have caused friction and frustration both inside and outside the schools and have largely prevented the secondary service from meeting adequately all the new demands created by the introduction of free secondary education for all.

Up to 1950 secondary school staffing problems did not receive the attention they warranted because the main official effort concentrated upon staving off the disaster threatening the primary schools. In the first few years after the war no urgent action was taken by the Department of Education to recruit more teachers for the secondary schools. Certainly there were grounds for believing that when the teachers were needed they would be available. In 1943 an authority on secondary education in New Zealand remarked that there was, 'even under present conditions, an ample supply of recruits for the secondary schools' (Murdoch, 1943, 270). Again, when in 1947, the Department of Education instituted a not very generous Post-Primary Teacher Bursary scheme to encourage university graduates to enter secondary teaching, there were 203 applications for the 65 bursaries. In the following year 264 students applied for 55 bursaries. In 1949, the Director of Education, anxious to avoid a repetition of the primary staffing crisis at the secondary level, asked the government to approve the award of 100 bursaries in 1950; instead it approved 40. In 1950 he asked for 300 bursaries but was allowed only half that number. Thereafter the director asked for fewer bursaries and his requests were usually granted without much quibbling because it had become apparent that the birth-rate was continuing to rise.

The parsimony of the government in 1950 and 1951 was extremely ill-timed. Had the bursary quotas approved then been more generous, or had a scheme similar to that introduced in 1956 been initiated earlier, when competition for graduates in business and industry was less keen, at least 200 to 300 more teachers might have been recruited. The government's error of judgment at this critical time probably derived from two factors: the suspicion with which the Minister of Education in the new National administration—the Labour Government had been defeated in the general elections of 1949 after fourteen years in office—regarded the director and all his works, and the failure of departmental staffing returns to give a clear picture of what was actually happening in the schools. They did not show, for example, that in many schools part-time teachers (often untrained and under-qualified) were employed; they gave little indication that district high schools were experiencing difficulties in attracting staff with the varied range of specialist skills so essential if country children were to have something approaching equality of educational opportunity; and they did not draw attention to the sharp decrease in the number of science graduates entering teaching even though, in girls' secondary schools, the dire shortage of women science teachers was already making difficult the provision of advanced level courses in chemistry, mathematics and physics.

At last the government recognized the inevitability of continuing staff shortages in the secondary schools, and agreed in 1956 to a new teacher recruitment scheme. A financially attractive Post-Primary Teacher Studentship was substituted for the Teacher Bursary. Under the new scheme studentship awards could be made at any stage in a student's university career, but by far the greatest number have been made to seventh formers who are then 'bonded' to teach for as many years as they have held the studentship. They may, of course, buy their way out of their contracts.

There has been criticism of the scheme ever since its inception. As early as 1959 the Committee on the New Zealand Universities recommended that all forms of bonded studentships be eliminated as soon as possible (Committee on New Zealand Universities, 1959, 45–6). The New Zealand University Students' Association has consistently maintained that the bonded studentship is an unethical method of recruitment because it offers something which appears attractive at a time when candidates are not really capable of deciding their future careers.

Persistent and often highly emotional criticism of its 'inefficient, cumbersome, repugnant and unnecessary' recruitment scheme (*Evening Post*, 25 March 1969), did not persuade the Department of Education to discontinue it in face of the almost insatiable demand for secondary school staff throughout the 1960s. As early as 1960 the Commission on Education spoke of 'an undeniable crisis in post-primary staffing' (Commission on Education, Interim Report, 1960, 7) and in 1968 the director-general reported that, although recruitment was just keeping pace with the increasing number of positions in all subjects, it was still not large enough to overtake the shortage (*A to J*, 1968, E–1, 17). Until the staffing situation improves, as it should in the 1970s, New Zealand secondary schools will continue to be unable to offer what the Minister of Education and his director sought in 1939, 'courses that are as rich and varied as are the needs and abilities of the children who enter them' (*A to J*, 1939, E–1, 3).

Achievements

A survey of two post-war decades of educational development in New Zealand must inevitably dwell on frustrations, deficiencies and vexations. It was a time of patching up, of making do, a time when, of necessity, the quantitative rather than the qualitative aspects of education were emphasized. After 1948 official references to the quality of the education system were few; always the stress was expansionist, and not until the department's 1964 report to parliament was this stress on quantity muted and emphasis placed once again on quality (*A to J*, 1964, E–1, 3).

The goals set by the Director of Education, A. E. Campbell, in 1964 were almost exactly those of his predecessor, C. E. Beeby, in 1946: smaller classes; better trained teachers; a wider variety of courses and a broadening and deepening of the curriculum at every stage. This was some indication of the consistency and continuity of departmental outlook and policy. The enlightened objectives in 1946, as the department's submissions to the Commission on Education showed clearly, constituted the basis for the limited amount of innovation and forward planning undertaken by the department during the crisis-ridden 1950s. The ground was prepared for more extensive pre-school services by a consultative committee which reported in 1947. Another consultative committee —it was the heyday of such committees—suggested how the quality of primary teacher-training could be improved without adding the luxury of a third year. More provision was made for the education of the handicapped. Indeed, in New Zealand where, unlike England, special education is the responsibility of education authorities alone, rather than one shared with health authorities, most of the extensive services now provided in special schools, classes and clinics have been established since 1945. A free textbook scheme was introduced in 1958; a wider range of reading materials was made available through school library services and the bulletins, journals and textbooks produced by the School Publications Branch of the Department of Education. Supporting services linking the home and the school were developed or extended. In these, and many other ways, the department showed its determination not to lose sight of what, through necessity, had become long-term plans for the improvement of the education system.

No one did more than C. E. Beeby, during his twenty years as director, to ensure that the liberal educational objective set out in the annual report to parliament of the Minister of Education in 1939 was not forgotten by administrators and planners in the hectic post-war years. This is hardly surprising; Beeby himself, then assistant-director, almost certainly had a hand in writing the relevant and much quoted section of the report which contains the objective. An astonishingly energetic, imaginative and sensitive administrator, Beeby quietly but surely, often in the face of strong public criticism, reconstructed and modernized the national education system. It was largely because of his vision and the dedication of his senior administrators that the Commission on Education could report to the government in 1962 that it believed the New Zealand system of education a good one, and in some respects an advanced one which compared not unfavourably with those in other leading countries in the western world (Commission on Education, 1962, 6). To its general commendation, however, the commission could have appended a critical note: that the process of modernization had led to an excessive accretion of power at the centre. Under Beeby's gifted leadership the dangers of such centralization were minimized or, as some would have it, concealed: under less capable or less respected direction the potential for friction and discontent within the education service could be considerable.

8

Change at the primary level

In the twenty-five years after the war the percentage of sole-charge schools dropped dramatically (from 43·5 per cent of all primary schools to 13·4 per cent) while the percentage of larger schools (ten or more classes) grew from 10 to 30 per cent. During this period the number of intermediate schools catering for the eleven- to thirteen-year-old groups increased from 26 to 109. By 1972 these schools enrolled nearly 60 per cent of all Form I–II pupils. Intermediate schools are intended to be able, through their accommodation, equipment and staffing, to offer better educational facilities than can be offered in eight-year primary schools.

Two-year intermediate schools have been the centre of educational controversy ever since 1933 when they replaced the experimental three-year junior high schools first established in 1922. Opponents argue that they cause an unnecessary break in children's schooling, that if primary schools cannot provide adequately for the needs of their older pupils then secondary education in New Zealand should follow the trend overseas and begin two years earlier. Supporters counter by asserting that the 'break' critics complain about is more apparent than real, that changing schools in company with their classmates stimulates rather than distresses children; they maintain that only in large, specialist staffed, separate schools can the wide range of interests and abilities of senior primary pupils be provided for satisfactorily.

Some spokesmen for the primary teachers see the intermediate school as the capstone of the primary structure, making primary teaching a more attractive career, especially for men. They reject outright the suggestion that Forms I and II be everywhere absorbed by the secondary schools although they are less opposed to the establishment of secondary schools with Forms I and II in rural areas where there are too few pupils to justify intermediate schools. To back up their case for separate Form I and II schools they cite the favourable findings of two comprehensive studies on intermediate

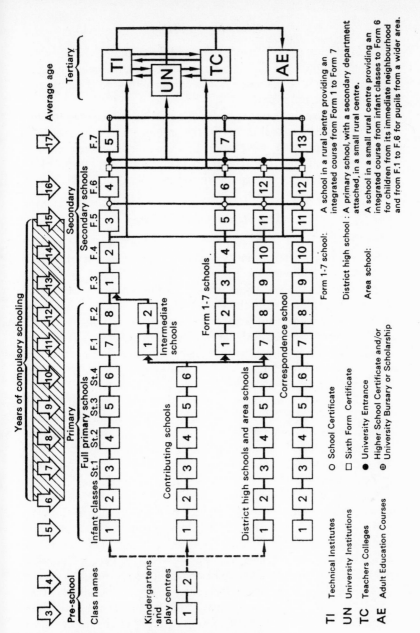

Figure 3   The New Zealand education system
(Source: Department of Education)

109

schools (Beeby, 1938; Watson, 1964) and the recommendation of the Commission on Education in 1962 that 'the present system of inter- mediate schools be extended in the cities and towns' (Commission on Education, 1962, 223).

While it is difficult to determine the relative influence of teacher politics and educational theory in the arguments mounted on both sides, it is clear that, with more than a hundred of them already established, intermediate schools are assured of a permanent place in the New Zealand pattern of primary schooling.

The primary curriculum

New Zealand is one of the few democratic countries in the post-war world where a central authority prescribes an official programme for every school. Although the 1964 Education Act did not, in contrast to the Acts of 1877 and 1914, actually list the subjects to be taught, it nevertheless reserved to the Department of Education the right to prescribe the studies and activities of state primary schools. Critics of the centrally-prescribed curriculum claim that it makes New Zealand's primary schools unnecessarily uniform and denies teachers the professional freedom enjoyed by their colleagues in the United States and England. Although this may have been true in the past, New Zealand teachers now have considerable responsibility for designing, within a broad framework, their class and school pro- grammes. Schools often devise 'schemes of work' markedly different from one another. The official syllabuses on which these are based are in turn the product of close consultation between the Department of Education and its teachers (Ewing, 1970, 208–58).

Changes in the primary programme have always been gradual and evolutionary, with each revision trying to point up current thinking and good practice in the light of developments in England, Scotland and the United States. More and more since 1945, in New Zealand as elsewhere, planners have been seeking to devise a curriculum that helps children 'to understand more about their society and its values, that gives them more scope for initiative and responsibility, that assists them to think more effectively and independently, that gives them more experience and skill in working together, that brings them into living touch with the great creative traditions of science and craftsmanship, poetry and drama, music and art' (Campbell, 1957, 9).

Consequently, the New Zealand primary programme is not unlike that of junior schools in England and elementary schools in the United States and Canada. In the infant classes, 'primers', emphasis is on reading and arithmetic but music and movement, drama and story all have a place in the daily programme. Time is also set aside for nature study, painting, crayon-drawing and simple craft-work. In the six classes beyond the primers a little over half the school week of twenty-five hours is devoted to English and mathematics, the teaching of which underwent radical change in the 1960s. Other subjects given prominence include: social studies, still largely a linking of history and geography; nature study and science; physical education and organized games; music and art and crafts of various kinds and health education in the syllabus for which sex is mentioned for the first time anywhere in the primary school curriculum. (Reflecting the caution of officialdom, the relevant passage affirms, 'there is no place in the primary school for group or class instruction on sex education'.) For boys in Forms I and II there is 'Handcraft in Wood and Metal' and for senior girls, 'Homecraft'. In 1965, after the department had refused for many years to approve a second language as a primary subject, French became an option for abler pupils of Form II in intermediate schools and six years later optional Maori was introduced in districts where it is taught in neighbouring secondary schools.

Curriculum development

Before the war revision of the primary school programme was the responsibility of departmental officers but after 1945 teachers and teachers' organizations were deliberately encouraged to participate more in curriculum reconstruction. At the same time the secondary school curriculum underwent changes intended to co-ordinate primary and secondary school studies but failed because the department had no specialist staff to oversee and facilitate the co-ordination. To remedy this, the Commission on Education recommended that permanent professional officers and an administrative staff in the department should be appointed to form the nucleus of a Curriculum Development Unit to keep under review the school curriculum from the infant classes to the sixth forms.

The unit was formed in 1963. Since then, curriculum revision committees, representative of all branches of the education service (including the independent schools, the universities and 'informed members of the public') have worked out a number of linked syllabuses for Forms I–IV which, while making it possible to teach certain subjects and concepts at an earlier stage than before, also prevent needless repetition of learning, omissions of knowledge that may be required later, and inconsistencies in teaching approaches. The unit is also responsible, either alone or in association with the department's School Publications Branch, for preparing guidelines and up-to-date teaching materials for the new courses. The Curriculum Development Unit has, in its few years of existence, gone some distance towards developing a national curriculum as distinct from a set of syllabuses. Each subject area is being developed on the basis of a common pattern involving the statement of precise objectives in terms of intended changes in pupils' cognitive and effective behaviour, the drafting of learning materials designed to achieve these objectives, the trial and appraisal of these materials in schools and then revision in the light of the trials prior to publication and dissemination. This is the process which, in its various forms, is in New Zealand as elsewhere, termed, 'curriculum development'.

The current work and potential of the unit are not generally appreciated by teachers. Appreciation would perhaps increase if it played a greater part in co-ordinating the curricular activities of other bodies such as the New Zealand Educational Institute, a pioneer in this area, the Post-Primary Teachers' Association, the New Zealand Council for Educational Research, the inspectorate and national examination boards.

Special education and auxiliary services

Compulsory education lasts from six to fifteen (98 per cent begin at five) but some children, because of physical, intellectual or emotional difficulties, are unable to benefit fully from regular classroom instruction. In New Zealand, as in England, the term 'special education' is used to describe the wide array of services assisting such children most of whom are of primary school age though, where appropriate the services have been extended to meet the needs of children at the pre-school and secondary stages. New Zealand practice separates handicapped children less than in England and educates them, as far as possible, in ordinary schools—an approach based on American practice. 'A separate day or residential school is provided', the department stresses, 'only when it is beyond the capacity of the ordinary schools to care effectively for a child' (Department of Education, Public Relations Section, 1968, 1).

As a result parents co-operate well with the educational authorities. Legally the Department of Education can direct handicapped and disturbed children into an appropriate special school, class or clinic but in actual practice this power has rarely been exercised. Parents usually accept the advice and recommendations of the department's psychologists, most of whom are former teachers. A psychological examination precedes admission to special classes and to reading or speech-training clinics.

The most numerous of the special classes—the first was established in 1917—are for backward children. There are also special primary school classes for the physically handicapped, for the partially sighted and the partially deaf, for children in hospital and for emotionally disturbed children. Many secondary schools are developing facilities for slow learners in 'vocational classes' which combine work experience with formal schooling and an increasing proportion—the number is growing at the rate of ten a year—have guidance counsellors to provide a link between home and school and to help children whose behaviour or lack of academic progress is a matter of concern to the class teachers. Primary teachers can ask a 'visiting teacher' with wide experience of day-to-day school problems to help. Such teachers are, in effect, educational social workers.

Special classes in public schools for children with severe hearing disabilities are recent. Until the beginning of the 1960s most hard-of-hearing children unable to make satisfactory progress at school were enrolled at one or other of two schools for the deaf, partly because of inherent difficulties in teaching them but mainly because the numbers of deaf children in any one town were too small to warrant a special class. An epidemic of rubella in expectant mothers in 1963–4, however, led to a sharp increase in the numbers of partially deaf children. In preparation for their arrival in primary school, provision for special classes was made in many centres.

Some separate schooling does have to be provided. The two residential schools for the deaf were opened late last century; two boarding schools for backward children were established early in this century. Special schools for emotionally disturbed children and for sufferers from cerebral palsy, on the other hand, are little more than a decade old. Mentally retarded children between five and eighteen who cannot benefit from special classes but who can live at home and be trained in the simpler physical, personal and social skills and habits, attend occupation centres controlled by education boards. The programme of a typical centre includes speech, hand-work, music and movement, story-telling, gardening, practical crafts and instruction in simple personal and domestic skills. To set up an occupation centre a minimum enrolment of twelve is necessary, but government financial support is available to parent-organized groups of five or more.

Intellectually severely handicapped children are looked after at no expense to their parents in special hospitals of the Department of Health. The Department of Education appoints teachers to the schools which have been opened in each of the hospitals. And from 1925–72, through the main national social work agency in the field of child care, its Child Welfare Division (now transferred to a new Department of Social Welfare), the Department of Education was responsible for training centres, 'open' institutions for the re-habilitation of wayward boys and girls.

Responsibility for the physical well-being of primary school children rests with the Department of Health. The Department's School Dental Service provides free treatment for pre-school and primary school children in clinics built in the grounds of the larger primary schools or in the mobile clinics in which dental nurses make six monthly visits to isolated country schools. The work of these specially trained nurses is essentially preventive dentistry, and includes the examination, cleaning and filling of teeth and, when necessary, simple extractions. Secondary school pupils up to the age of eighteen have their teeth cared for by private dentists at the state's expense. When the service was initiated in 1923 dental surgeons were sceptical but now they fully support it. The service has won international recognition and similar schemes have been organized in other countries. A second service, the School Medical Service, regularly checks the health of all pre-school and primary children. Holidays at 'health camps' have been offered since 1928 to delicate or undernourished children. Malnutrition is not now common among New Zealand school children but an increasing number of them with other problems, especially minor emotional difficulties, go to health camps where they attend a camp school. Since 1929 the costs of health camps have been defrayed by an annual sale of special health stamps.

The teaching profession

After 1945 the popularity of primary teaching as a career for men decreased, partly because of the many other employment opportunities which post-war technological and social changes opened up, and partly because the status of the male primary teacher in the community appeared to decline (Congalton and Havighurst, 1954). For women, on the other hand, equal pay made teaching more attractive. Between 1953 and 1958 50 per cent of the country's primary teachers were men but by 1968 the percentage had dropped to 39. Yet for men as well as for women teaching is not ill-paid. Further, the New Zealand teacher enjoys security of tenure and a high degree of social and civic freedom; he is well protected both by law and by his professional organizations which the Department of Education consults on matters affecting teachers. And by an arrangement probably unique to New Zealand, a representative of the New Zealand Educational Institute is always one of the three members of education board appointment committees.

These committees have little latitude because a teacher's eligibility for appointment is largely determined by his place on the 'grading scale'. Grading, a homespun system of merit rating or assessment on a nation-wide basis, is carried out by inspectors, all of whom are officers of the Department of Education recruited from the teaching service.

Visiting educationists often express surprise that local teachers continue to acquiesce in what appears to them to be a very unprofessional procedure. But the fact is that teachers themselves have clung tenaciously to the system as the only way of ensuring that the conscientious and hard-working teacher is recognized. The Department of Education has done much in recent years to modify and liberalize both the primary and secondary teacher classification schemes and is not a strong supporter of grading. When in 1969 a majority of secondary teachers voted in favour of abolishing the grading system altogether, the Minister of Education hailed the result 'as a major step forward' (*Evening Post*, 30 August 1969). However, a similar referendum among the more grading-conscious primary teachers is unlikely yet to give a similar result.

The Department of Education's post-war distaste for grading stems largely from its dislike of the educational policemen image projected by its primary and secondary inspectorates, an image which does not fairly reflect the scope and nature of their work which includes membership of innumerable departmental, education board or regional office committees; assisting teachers and schools with curriculum planning, a function which becomes of increasing importance as the syllabuses become more broadly defined; initiating or encouraging local in-service training ventures and, most important of all, providing the only direct link between the department on the one hand and local authorities and the schools on the other. In New Zealand, as in England, 'a good inspectorate is an essential personal link between a distant department and the people involved in its administration' (Leese, 1950, 5).

In-service training

'In-service training' covers all activities that help practising teachers to broaden their view of their professional responsibilities and to carry them out more efficiently. Since 1944, teachers' national organizations have helped to arrange summer vacation courses for their members. The Department of Education, which appointed an Officer for In-Service Training in 1953, has also become increasingly active; it opened its first permanent residential in-service training centre in 1961 and its second in 1971. In education board non-residential centres, assistance is given to classroom teachers through workshop courses and seminars arranged by branches of the teachers' associations with the encouragement and help of the inspectorate. Since the mid-1960s relieving teachers have been employed to free teachers to attend these courses; in 1972, 1 per cent of the teaching force was so freed. A national advisory committee, set up in 1961 and representative of the department and the teachers, attempts to co-ordinate local and national effort. The universities, although they contribute little directly to the organization and provision of in-service training, do play a major part indirectly, by admitting practising teachers to their degree and diploma courses on a part-time or extramural basis. In 1961 the Department of Education, impressed by the willingness of many teachers, particularly primary, to improve their qualifications introduced, through the Correspondence School, its own extramural Diploma in Teaching. The emphasis in this has been described, perhaps prophetically, as being on 'professional content which could be developed into a prescription if a teachers' degree were instituted' (Supervisor, Diploma in Teaching Course, 1966). The enthusiasm teachers have shown for the Department's diploma (1,200 teachers a year take one or other of the ten courses available) and their readiness to spend time, effort and money to attend local and national in-service training courses (many more apply to attend than there are places available), reflect their increasing acceptance of in-service work as an essential part of a teacher's further professional training and growth.

Not enough is yet being done for teachers. The reconstruction of the curriculum along modern lines makes heavy demands upon them, particularly as it is now realized the curriculum must be continually modified to keep it in step with the constantly changing needs of pupils and society as well as with the rapid growth of knowledge. The existing advisory services provided by the department to support teachers are proving inadequate. The need for a massive increase in the provision of in-service training and better resource facilities at local and regional levels is urgent. Universities, teachers' colleges and every kind of professional association must be involved.

9

Secondary education: characteristics, problems and prospects

Since 'proficiency', the primary school leaving examination, was abolished in 1936 and the school-leaving age was raised to fifteen in 1945, New Zealand state secondary schools have catered for the whole range of the adolescent population and become multi-course institutions. One reason is that in a still sparsely-populated country the needs of a whole district must frequently be met by one secondary school, but the main reason is that most New Zealanders believe the social advantages of bringing together all the children of a community and emphasizing their common needs, outweigh the disadvantage that in doing so the scholastic achievement of a very able minority may suffer. 'The preference in New Zealand for a multi-lateral type of secondary school,' the Commission on Education observed in 1962, 'is too marked for any educational administration to ignore, and the Commission sees no really strong educational reason to recommend anything other than what the country so evidently wants' (Commission on Education, 1962, 12).

Secondary schools, although variously termed grammar schools, high schools, colleges, technical high schools, technical colleges and agricultural colleges, have become remarkably similar since 1945. They are all unselective, they are all governed by the same regulations, given the same grants, staffed by teachers trained in the same teachers' colleges, cover the same length of schooling and are inspected by Department of Education officers. They all teach practically the same subjects and prepare pupils for the same national examinations. Schools differ very little in organization and administration; even their buildings are frequently replicas of one another.

The degree of uniformity can be overstressed, however. A number of schools have certain distinguishing features. Some, for example, have their own farms. Older city schools, many of them nineteenth-century foundations, still manage to preserve their pre-war aura of academic superiority. Former technical schools, although now fully comprehensive, usually offer a wider range of technical options than other schools. While most secondary schools are co-educational, about one-fifth of the 200 or so are single-sex. But the chief defence of the secondary schools against becoming stereotyped state institutions is provided by their boards of governors which, although circumscribed in their powers, contribute much towards the individuality and character of their schools.

The university influence

Before the Education (Post-Primary Instruction) Regulations of 1945 made a 'core' of general subjects compulsory for all pupils, and the School Certificate Examination replaced the University Entrance Examination 'as the ordinary measure of a satisfactory secondary education' (*A to J*, 1948, E–1, 4) New Zealand secondary schools were, with a few notable exceptions, narrowly academic institutions, a characteristic imprinted by the stranglehold of the University Entrance Examination or, more popularly, 'Matric', on the work of the secondary schools. Originally intended as a prerequisite for university studies, this examination came to serve also as a general leaving qualification. In 1945, when 65 per cent of primary school leavers were going on to secondary school, nearly 75 per cent of secondary pupils were taking the highly academic course leading to 'Matric' even though only eight pupils out of every hundred entering a secondary school actually went on to enrol at a university college.

To reduce the influence of its entrance examination the Senate of the University of New Zealand agreed, in 1944, to modify admission arrangements to allow principals of secondary schools approved by the university and the Department of Education to recommend for university admission sixth form pupils with satisfactory attainment in English and three other subjects. Pupils not so 'accredited' by their schools, and those from schools not given an accrediting status could still qualify for entrance by passing the university's own external examination run at the end of each school year.

This compromise, reached after years of argument, has, like most compromises, aroused misgivings and on one occasion a majority of secondary teachers voted to abolish it. There is now, however, general agreement among secondary and university teachers that the principle of accrediting is sound; most agree with the 1959 judgment of the Committee on New Zealand Universities that it could see 'no reason why accrediting for University Entrance should be rejected' (Committee on New Zealand Universities, 1959, 27). The introduction of accrediting cleared the way for a thorough-going revision of the secondary curriculum and, by making the university entrance course a four-instead of a three-year one, allowed the Department of Education's School Certificate Examination (in existence, but languishing, since 1934) to establish itself as the general leaving qualification.

Continued university acceptance of accrediting depends upon the maintenance of school standards; the universities must be confident that principals and staff can judge who among their sixth formers will enjoy reasonable success at university. To help them determine standards university-appointed liaison officers check the university progress of all accredited students and report their findings to the schools. If necessary, schools must then raise or lower their accrediting standards.

Criticisms

Academic secondary schools before the war tended to be highly authoritarian and more suited to serve a hierarchical society than the egalitarian one in which they actually existed. Only when the school-leaving age was raised were secondary school teachers brought face to face with reality.

Many of their pretensions and much of their insularity were destroyed but not everyone agrees they have yet adapted fully to post-1945 circumstances. One of their earliest critics, the iconoclastic Professor D. P. Ausubel, challenger of many cherished and comfortable New Zealand beliefs, told a conference of Department of Justice psychologists in 1958 that 'the secondary school system impresses the overseas visitor as the most anachronistic segment of New Zealand educational life' (Ausubel, 1958, 12). He ascribed to the secondary schools major responsibility for the undesirable adolescent behaviour which had led in 1954 to a Special Committee on Moral Delinquency in Children and Adolescents, a copy of whose very general but disturbing report was sent to every household. Ausubel held that the unnecessarily repressive discipline of the schools, the militaristic atmosphere of boys' schools, the exaggerated deference to teachers and principals expected of pupils, the use of corporal punishment, insistence on school uniforms, the prefect system, all contributed to anti-social behaviour outside the school and to the growth of the 'bodgie-widgie' cult (the New Zealand equivalent of the 'Teddy boy' cult in England). 'It is still taken for granted by many parents and teachers', he claimed, 'that the traditional policies to which they were accustomed are absolutely essential for the orderly operation of a post-primary school' (ibid.).

Ausubel's comments together with his tersely expressed views on Maori–Pakeha relations, were unpalatable to many New Zealanders in spite of their substantial accuracy. Both the Hunn Report in 1960 and the report two years later of the Commission on Education, acknowledged, implicitly rather than explicitly, the validity of a number of Ausubel's assertions about race relations and secondary education. The commission's agreement was qualified. It pointed to a common tendency among those seeking to reform New Zealand secondary schools 'to exaggerate past authoritarianism and to forget much of the benevolence and kindliness which often tempered the autocracy of earlier regimes in classroom and school' (Commission on Education, 1962, 299). The commission, however, was aware that all was not well with secondary education, and that its problems were more likely to increase than decrease in the future.

Problems

After 1945 the secondary service, like the primary, was short of staff and accommodation. In addition, changed conceptions of secondary education gave rise to other problems. Many teachers, accustomed to the semi-selective, pre-war system, found it hard to adjust to universal secondary education. They could not see the secondary school, as they knew it, in a new light, as a new kind of institution doing a new kind of job.

Secondary schools generally—with some exceptions—were slow to adapt. Children in the lower-ability groups were all too often foisted upon the least experienced teachers who seldom knew how to initiate them into what, to many, seemed an alien and hostile world. Only when teachers qualified by experience and temperament to work with the slower learners were given positions of responsibility did the lot of the less able pupils begin to improve. Even now, there is still a tendency in some schools to equate intellectual status with human worth; for too many lower-ability children, secondary school remains a confused and confusing place. They resent their low status, are clearly bored, are unco-operative in and outside the classroom and become members of notorious gangs. Yet recent experience has shown that the interests, enthusiasm and co-operation of most of these slower learners can be captured by the right teachers and suitable courses. Less amenable are the reluctant learners who tend to be defensive and suspicious; usually, but not always, they have limited ability and attend school on sufferance. They do not want to learn and appear to delight in disruptive behaviour. For the young teacher these children are probably the greatest single source of strain and frustration.

In an increasing number of urban secondary schools Polynesian children constitute a third category of pupils whose presence was barely noticed before 1945 but who now pose, some teachers consider, 'a disciplinary problem, a teaching problem and eventually a drop-out problem' (*NZEI*, 1967, 12). A regrettably disproportionate number of Maori pupils in state secondary schools are found in the lower ability forms waiting impatiently for their fifteenth birthday when they can escape. Able Maori boys, admitted to the pre-apprenticeship training schemes organized by the Department of Maori Affairs, described their secondary schools as harsh and inhospitable, ruled over by teachers who made too ready use of the cane and frequently humiliated them. They complained that many lessons were difficult and irrelevant and said how bewildered they often were by the language and methods of instruction (Bates, 1970, 124).

Nevertheless the New Zealand secondary schools have provided reasonably well for almost all the school population within a framework originally devised for a selected minority. The schools have achieved more than mere victory over numbers. Philosophies and practices in education established in nineteenth-century British schools that had never been fundamentally challenged by classroom teachers in New Zealand were looked at afresh in the 1950s and their relevance to the New Zealand situation critically examined.

Consequently a peculiarly New Zealand institution has evolved in which the hard lines between general and vocational education have been blurred, and something approaching parity of esteem achieved, or at least aimed at, between academic and non-academic courses.

Evolution continues. By the early 1970s several secondary school practices and assumptions current a decade earlier had disappeared or altered. But probably the single most remarkable change was in the pupils themselves, particularly the over fifteens who now constitute half the secondary population. These young people have very different attitudes and outlook from the fifteen- to eighteen-year-olds of the immediate post-war period. In social comment and value judgments today's sixth and seventh formers rank with the adults of twenty-one, not with the children of thirteen. They refuse to accept without question the traditional values and practices of the secondary school. They resent attempts by their teachers, however benevolent, to treat them as children; they are restless and self-assertive; they want status and can become aggressive if thwarted in their efforts to achieve it as is clearly indicated by the spread of student unrest from the universities to the upper forms of secondary schools.

Teacher reaction to this new mood is varied. Almost all agree that some traditional relationships between teacher and taught, both inside and outside the classroom, should change and that senior pupils should be given more responsibility. However, not all agree that major reforms or sweeping innovations should be introduced when the staffing of so many schools is still less than adequate. Nevertheless change is taking place steadily if unspectacularly. Ausubel's strictures on corporal punishment, school uniforms and the prefect system no longer have the validity they had when made in 1958.

Corporal punishment, for example, is much less used but has by no means disappeared. The Department of Education is not prepared to legislate against corporal punishment, but periodically makes clear that for indiscipline more appropriate forms of punishment can be found. Not all principals and teachers—or parents for that matter—agree. They argue that corporal punishment is the only kind some pupils respect and that its total prohibition would further accelerate the downward trend of teacher morale. They are not prepared to have it banned in the schools until adequate guidance, counselling and psychological services (a national scheme of guidance services for secondary pupils was proposed by the Department of Education in 1971) are available to help teachers to identify and manage troublesome pupils. Yet everywhere, gradually, corporal punishment is disappearing from state secondary schools.

Also disappearing is the frequently criticized traditional school uniform. Once worn as a matter of course and often with some pride, the school uniform's desirability is now questioned by senior pupils and parents alike. Some governing bodies, having secured legal authority to enforce the wearing of school uniforms, insist that all pupils do so. Other authorities accept the new attitudes and make concessions as graciously as they can.

Concessions have also been made regarding school government. Many principals, stung by criticism of authoritarianism and of staff-appointed prefects have experimented with systems of pupil government designed to enlist the pupils' help and goodwill. 'Social revolution', one experienced teacher remarked, 'can be prevented only by social reform' (Meikle, 1961, 32). The day of the prefect system—once itself a major step forward in staff–pupil relations—is almost over in New Zealand. In an increasing number of schools, popularly elected school councils, with varying degrees of authority, are replacing the prefects.

Supply and training of teachers

Reform and innovation during the 1960s were seriously hindered because, in spite of efforts to recruit teachers both in New Zealand and overseas, many schools were inadequately staffed for most of the decade. To retain teachers, as much as to recruit them, has been a major difficulty. Through its university studentship scheme and special short-term training courses, the department attracted a reasonable number of young graduates into secondary teaching but many of these left in their first five years of service, often because of heavy work loads (the average New Zealand teacher teaches 30 or 31 periods during a 35-period week), over-large and unresponsive classes, or better salary offers from outside teaching. As a result the annual turnover rate among full-time secondary teachers in the 1960s was one in six. This serious loss of teachers also adversely affected recruitment. Senior pupils who saw young teachers driven out of teaching were understandably reluctant to enter an arduous profession of diminishing public esteem. The tide may, however, have turned in 1970 when a new salary scale and fewer openings for graduates in industry and the public service combined to make secondary teaching a more attractive career.

While the shortage of teachers generally is becoming less acute there is a continuing shortage of teachers of mathematics, chemistry and particularly of physics. The number of physics graduates at M.Sc. level completing their teacher training courses at the two secondary teachers' colleges in the years 1965-9 were: 1965, 2; 1966, 2; 1967, 0; 1968, 1; 1969, 3.

The route into secondary teaching is quite distinct from that into primary teaching. Most prospective secondary teachers attend university full-time on Department of Education studentships which pay tuition fees and provide adequate cost-of-living allowances for up to five years. On completing their university courses all studentship holders are required to undertake a one-year course of training, the requirements for which are very similar to those in England for the Post-Graduate Certificate of Education, at either Auckland Secondary Teachers' College, established in 1964, or the separate secondary division of Christchurch Teachers' College. Graduates who have not held studentships are also accepted for this one-year training programme as are considerable numbers of students with incomplete degrees who continue their university studies concurrently with their college work. An important development in secondary teacher training was the introduction of the three-year concurrent university and teachers' college courses for teachers of general subjects. Efforts to recruit graduates of an older age group through a three-month trial period of teaching have also met with some success.

As well as graduate teachers of the traditional academic subjects, the multi-course New Zealand secondary schools also require large numbers of qualified teachers of music, homecraft, physical education, woodwork and metalwork and commercial subjects. Special training schemes have been developed at one or more teachers' colleges to attract into teaching men and women with skills in these areas.

Quality of teachers and teaching

The proportion of graduates among secondary school teachers decreased steadily in the post-war years. In 1950, 36·8 per cent of the permanent full-time teachers had a master's degree; in 1965 the percentage had dropped to 30·4 and in 1967 it was down to 27·8. The proportion of teachers with first degrees declined too, dashing the hopes of the Post-Primary Teachers' Association that secondary teaching would become an all-graduate profession. Many non-graduate secondary teachers are, however, excellent for general subjects and those with experience in primary schools are often more able than many graduate teachers to understand the needs and interests of the non-academic third of the secondary school population. Much more serious than the increase in non-graduate teachers is the inadequacy or incompetency of many teachers—not uncommonly graduates—taken on in the absence of other applicants. The number of such teachers in the secondary service at the end of the 1960s was estimated at 10 per cent (Jackman, 1969). From time to time, schools, even in cities, are quite unable to fill a vacancy and are forced to enrol the classes affected (including classes in subjects requiring laboratory work) with the Department of Education's Correspondence School in Wellington.

Standards of work have declined in the worst affected schools. In some, basic courses are not available in the lower forms and even core subjects may exist in name only. (The slipshod teaching of core mathematics is a particular cause for worry.) Pupils' chances of entering certain professions, of following certain careers, are jeopardized because they cannot be given the essential preliminary tuition. Many girls are particularly disadvantaged because of the long-standing shortage of well qualified science and mathematics teachers in girls' schools.

The increasing dependence of secondary schools during the 'crisis years' upon anyone who was available threw an added burden upon full-time teachers. Married women, who make up a growing proportion of the part-time force, have family responsibilities which limit the time they have for preparation, marking and, of course, extra-classroom activities; similarly, superannuitants, the other sizeable group among relieving teachers, are seldom willing to share extra-curricular responsibilities. Timetables had to be adapted to accommodate part-time teachers. Not surprisingly the efficiency and enthusiasm of competent permanent staff declined and their sense of frustration and helplessness increased. Occasionally a teacher gave vent publicly to opinions usually reserved for the staff-room. 'The entire present generation of our secondary school population', a member of the Post-Primary Teachers' Association executive said, 'is suffering educational deprivation of dismaying proportions' (*Evening Post*, 20 August 1968).

Such comment, together with neighbourhood gossip, has increased parental disquiet about the quality of education in the state secondary schools. Confidence in their ability to give specialist academic tuition to a minority of pupils, and a sound general education to the majority, has been eroded. Reluctantly, some parents, who a few years ago would never have entertained the idea, now send their children to private secondary schools where they believe a better all-round education is offered.

This view is fairly widely held but it is not substantiated by hard evidence. Private secondary schools also find it difficult to recruit qualified teachers. The fact that they are smaller than the typical urban state secondary schools does not necessarily guarantee smaller classes or greater individual attention. As fee-charging institutions they have their share of difficult pupils and reluctant learners. Most private schools are non-selective—they have to be to survive financially—so they have the same mixture of able and not-so-able, ill-behaved and well-behaved pupils as state schools.

The noticeable movement of pupils from state schools to private schools is not yet a cause for alarm. It would become significant, however, if diminishing public confidence in the state secondary school system should coincide with greatly increased state support for an independent school system.

Curriculum and examinations

Much needed curriculum reforms in secondary education were made possible by the introduction of accrediting for university entrance. Raising the school-leaving age to fifteen a year later made reform urgently necessary. The groundwork had already been laid in 1943 in the report of a consultative committee, the Thomas Committee, whose recommendations the Department of Education embodied in its *Education (Post-Primary Instruction) Regulations* of 1945 which led to a major curriculum reorganization and ended the domination of university requirements. The regulations have been hailed as 'New Zealand's most significant post-war educational reform' (Ewing, 1970, 207).

The report of the Thomas Committee was progressive and realistic and took into account not only the intellectual, but also the moral, social and aesthetic purposes in education. Its terms of reference required the committee to consider the choice and content of subjects for one national external examination, the School Certificate. The committee went further and offered a curriculum blueprint it hoped would ensure 'all post-primary pupils, irrespective of their varying occupational ambitions . . . a generous and well-balanced education' (Department of Education, 1959, 5).

At the heart of the proposed curriculum was a 'common core' containing what the committee suggested any intelligent parent might expect his son or daughter to be given at school: a course in physical education; an adequate command of the mother tongue and an ability to enjoy something of its literature; an understanding of the pupils' environment in time and space; a knowledge of the mathematics required for ordinary non-school purposes; some appreciation of the methods and achievements of science; an ability to listen intelligently to music; and some aptitude in an art or craft. Regulations based on the Thomas Committee's recommendations prescribed a minimum number of hours a week for each of these subjects or groups of subjects. The completion of a stated number of such units of instruction over a period of three years was made a prerequisite for entry to the fifth form School Certificate Examination which, once the University Entrance Examination had been made a sixth form one, became a keenly sought-after qualification.

The School Certificate Examination regulations were simple. At least a three-year preliminary secondary school course was required (the Thomas Committee's recommendation that the course leading up to the examination be a four-year one for most pupils was largely ignored); a maximum of five subjects could be taken and for success a pass in four, of which English had to be one, was needed. Candidates were required to obtain a minimum of 30 per cent in each of the four subjects and a total mark of at least 200. Because the intention of the School Certificate Examination was—and is—that it should give a large number of children of differing abilities and interests opportunity for success at school, it embraces a heterogeneous collection of over thirty options.

The attempt to combine a general education programme with one leading to a national examination was foredoomed to failure. Inevitably examination requirements soon began to dominate the work of all classes, even those in which there were few potential examination candidates. Before long schools were shackled once again in the examination fetters that the Thomas Committee had tried so hard to rid them of.

Criticism of the School Certificate Examination has mounted steadily over the years even though its retention has been justified by the Commission on Education as well as by two specially appointed review committees. Critics say the examination looms too large in the estimation of children, parents and employers and has come, as the University Entrance Examination before it, to define the meaning and purpose of secondary education. It stultifies teacher initiative, usurps control over the curriculum, puts a premium on cramming and encourages dull teaching. The justice of these claims can be questioned. Some teaching would be dull regardless of external examinations. School Certificate Examination syllabuses give room for teachers to be interesting and stimulating. More to the point are the criticisms that examination standards are too high for the dull, too low for the able, and that for an increasing number of candidates success or failure is based not on ability but whether they are lucky enough to have good teachers in their School Certificate year. Public scepticism is further heightened by the knowledge that the Department of Education, by a process of scaling, deliberately maintains a fixed percentage of passes— approximately 50 per cent—each year.

The Department of Education, aware that the opponents of the School Certificate Examination are more vocal than its defenders, has declined to abandon it, arguing that it provides a yardstick against which pupils and teachers can measure their own performances; it affords some kind of continuing national assessment of the education system; it gives an indication (a surprisingly accurate one in fact) of likely future academic success and it is of use to the business community. However, in 1967 the department tacitly acknowledged the validity of some of the criticism and

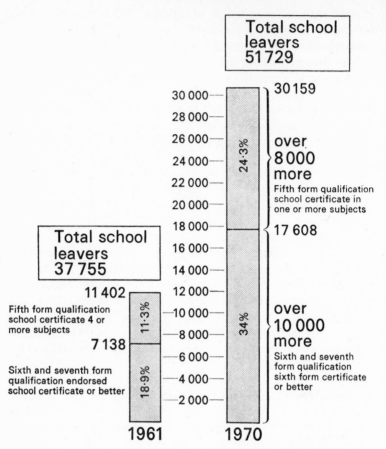

Figure 4 Attainments of secondary school leavers, 1961–70
(Source: Department of Education)

changed the School Certificate Examination by substituting single subject passes (up to a maximum of six) for the previously required group pass in English and three other subjects. (This extended the practice begun in 1961 of awarding Certificates of Education to candidates who failed to obtain a full School Certificate but who passed in one or more subjects.) The new style School Certificate Examination, with English no longer a compulsory subject, designed to challenge able pupils and to be more attainable for those of modest capacity, replaced the old in 1969. The effect of this change on the retention rate, especially for girls, has been noteworthy. In 1971 48 per cent of both boys and girls who had entered secondary schools in 1968 were in their fourth year compared with 35 per cent and 31 per cent respectively ten years earlier (Department of Education, 1972, 14). In response to the marked growth in senior school enrolments (state secondary school enrolments rose 18 per cent overall between 1966 and 1972, those of sixth and seventh formers 60 per cent) and the consequent increase in the number of pupils not wishing to take Universities Entrance Board examinations, the Department of Education replaced its undemanding Endorsed School Certificate with an internally-assessed, single subject Sixth Form Certificate.

Course structures

The Department of Education, accepting the Thomas Committee's view that the state should not impose a cut-and-dried philosophy on the schools by controlling the curriculum in detail, set out a very broad and flexible basis for secondary school courses. The details were left to the schools and the teachers.

This latitude has not led to any great variety in the courses offered. Most schools place the more able of their new entrants (ability is assessed on the basis of primary school record and performance in a series of school-administered entrance tests), in a course variously styled academic, professional, or general, which includes one or two foreign languages and mathematics in addition to the core subjects. The nature of the specialist options in other courses is almost always indicated by their titles: commercial, industrial, home life, agricultural.

Because all courses contain a high proportion of common core subjects the classification of pupils on entry to secondary school and the placing of them in particular courses is not too critical. Nevertheless, it is still important, since a pupil who is wrongly placed may find it difficult to change later from one course to another. Seriously misplaced pupils are, as a rule, detected by the end of their first term and then transferred. Cross-setting has also grown in popularity. This brings pupils together from a number of different courses and rearranges their groups according to ability in particular subjects.

Limits to this type of internal organization are set by the availability of teachers and timetabling difficulties.

In the fifth forms of many schools course structures are abandoned and pupils are grouped according to the options they are taking for the School Certificate Examination. This is possible because of the widespread practice of allotting more time to the core minima in social studies, general science, mathematics and English during the first two years at secondary school than regulations require. Although the Department of Education advocates a continued general education in the fifth, sixth and seventh forms, many secondary school principals are only gradually being persuaded to do more than pay lip-service to its ideal. Liberal or general studies courses personally relevant to senior pupils have been actively promoted by the Curriculum Development Unit for some time but principals are often reluctant to allow too radical departures from the orthodox and familiar topics of classroom debate. Many are nervous about the discussions likely to be stimulated by liberal studies courses. They doubt the neutrality of some of their teachers and, in particular, they fear that offence will be given to parents or politicians. In most sixth and seventh forms pupils concentrate upon the subjects they are taking for the University Entrance or University Bursaries Examinations. The variety of the combinations possible, as with cross-setting, is limited by staffing and timetabling, and subjects tend to be grouped in such ways as to make them appear separate courses.

The future

Reform and innovations in secondary education are likely to increase. They will probably fall into one or other of two main categories: those which can be carried out within the existing structure of the secondary schools and those which will depend upon major changes in the organization of secondary education. Of the former, the most likely major reform is a review of the overall structure of the curriculum, the shape and balance of which is beginning to be questioned at a time when the schools are being challenged to find ways of relating work to the needs, interests and concerns of pupils as they are now, while simultaneously maintaining the best from the past and preparing for the future. It is suggested that such a review be carried out by a National Committee for Secondary Education 'representative of all appropriate interests' (Curriculum Development Unit, 1972, 4).

Related to curriculum change is the question of the future of public examinations, especially the School Certificate. While there is some enthusiasm within the profession for internal assessment, the School Certificate Examination Board has not committed itself to such a policy and the public seems not to be in favour (*New Zealand Herald*, 3 March 1973).

A virtue of curricular and examination innovations is that they will not add greatly to the running costs of the system. Costs will, however, soar if the present organization of secondary education is altered significantly, as has been urged, to allow for the development of seventh-form colleges or community colleges serving a variety of local educational needs. It is claimed that in the more adult atmosphere which would pervade these institutions, seventeen- and eighteen-year-olds, so many of whom appear to have outgrown their secondary schools, would have better opportunities to equip themselves either to go on to further education or to enter employment. Guidance rather than selection would be the function of the new institutions which for some students would stand in the same relationship to tertiary education as intermediate schools currently do to secondary education. Seventh form colleges, dismissed by the Commission on Education in 1962, would be opposed by many vested interests. Nevertheless, some experimentation seems likely. Whatever the future, secondary schools must not be, as one fifteen-year-old pupil described them in Edward Blishen's *The School That I'd Like*, 'institutions of today run on the principles of yesterday'.

Developments in tertiary education

Since 1945, but especially after 1960, expansion at the tertiary level has been enormous with teachers' colleges, technical institutes and universities adding greatly to their numbers and to the depth and diversity of their courses.

Teacher education

Until the phased introduction of three-year primary teacher training in 1966, the teachers' colleges attempted, in two crowded years, to broaden the personal education of young students as well as to give them some insight into the aims of education, some knowledge of syllabus construction and of methods of teaching, and some experience in the classroom. In the event student teachers were frequently merely drilled in the elements of the primary school curriculum and little more. They found their college courses neither personally satisfying nor adequate to fit them, as the Minister of Education agreed in 1945, 'to meet all the demands of the modern primary school' (Mason, 1945, 67).

In 1946 the government approved in principle the introduction of three-year primary teacher training but the consultative committee set up two years later to report on the recruitment, education and training of teachers could not, because of spectacular increases in primary school enrolments, recommend a longer course of training. In its 1951 report in face of an acute primary teacher shortage when academic standards and personal acceptability for teacher training had been greatly relaxed, it suggested certain changes in college courses as palliatives. Of particular significance were recommendations that students should specialize in either junior or senior class teaching and that they should be required to study some subjects in much greater depth than hitherto.

More consultative and advisory committee reports followed and colleges experimented during the next few years. By 1959 there was enough agreement among them for the Department of Education to define in Teachers' Training College Regulations, minimum national requirements for primary teacher education. These, still the basis of teacher college courses, made compulsory the following studies: spoken and written English; the general theory of education and the principles and practice of teaching with special reference to either the five- to eight-year or the eight- to thirteen-year age group; the organization, social life, curriculum and teaching methods of either the junior (Infants to Standard 2) or senior (Standard 2 to Form II) school; physical education, health education and music. Each student's course had to include at least 400 hours of practical training involving child study, classroom observation and regular and co-ordinated practice teaching in local schools and in the normal and model country schools attached to each of the primary teachers' colleges. In addition, in accordance with the recommendations of the 1951 report, the Regulations required each student to select four optional or 'credit' subjects for intensive study. And following a long-standing tradition in teacher training in New Zealand, students qualified to matriculate were to be encouraged to substitute university courses for teachers' college credits.

Since 1965 particularly well-qualified teachers' college students (the percentage of entrants with university entrance rose from 45 per cent in 1960 to nearly 90 per cent in 1973) have been able to attend university full-time before beginning their professional training or after their first year at a teachers' college or at the end of their three-year college course. Graduates or near graduates may enrol for a one or two year programme. Typically, however, a student spends three years at a large co-educational college and in the fourth year is assigned to a school as a probationary assistant. After a satisfactory year's teaching the probationer is awarded a Trained Teacher's Certificate by the director-general. He or she can then apply for, and be appointed to, his or her first permanent position as a certificated teacher. Because they have been salaried during training all beginning teachers are bonded to teach for three years, a condition which causes some resentment among student teachers and considerable dissatisfaction in the teaching profession generally.

But in spite of this continuing irritant the 1970s are full of promise for teacher education following the most substantial programme of development in teacher training in New Zealand's history. Salaries of teachers' college staffs have been raised, the proportion of senior positions has been substantially increased, the staff–student ratio has changed from 1:18 to 1:16·5 and extension and rebuilding of the colleges is planned for completion by 1980. Now that the earlier need for quick expansion has eased, more attention is being given to the content, structure and organization of training and, as the academic calibre of teachers' college entrants improves, to college–university relationships. The establishment of a School of Education at the University of Waikato in 1966 led to a significant departure in the training of primary teachers. College and School co-operate closely in providing joint courses in some subjects and special courses in others, in addition to those taught at the University. The undergraduate programme of studies leads to an intermediate award, the Diploma of Education, normally completed in the three years at Hamilton Teachers' College. The Bachelor of Education degree requires a further year of full-time study although it is possible to undertake part-time study for both the degree and the diploma. Somewhat similar arrangements give credit towards a university qualification at Massey University and the University of Otago.

Technical and vocational education

Technical secondary schools were established in the first decade of this century because of the stubborn refusal of existing secondary schools to accede to requests from the Minister of Education and his department to adapt their 'courses of instruction so as to meet the needs of pupils for whom an education more or less literary in character would not afford the best training for their life-work'.

From the outset (the first day school was opened in 1905) the technical schools gave a secondary education with a practical bias and not, as was often the case in other countries, direct trade training. The evening vocational classes provided by all the technical schools and some secondary schools then, as now, were regarded as quite separate from, and subsidiary to, the full-time day schools. During the next forty years the technical schools became less distinctively technical and, especially after 1945, more like other multilateral schools.

As long as secondary industry was of minor importance the lack of specialized technical institutions was not serious; the pre-vocational courses in the technical day schools turned out pupils well fitted to take their place in a wide range of small, scattered and relatively simple industries. But the rapid growth of concentrated and complex industries after 1935—between 1935-6 and 1947-8 the volume of production of secondary industry increased by 86 per cent—made apparent the need for more specialized technical training directly preparing students for work in industry and commerce.

Demand was further accelerated by certain policy decisions. The 1948 Apprentices Act, for example, made it compulsory for apprentices to undertake technical classes, point and direction to which were given by the creation of the Trades Certification Board and national trades examinations. Students flooded into the technical schools in Auckland, Wellington, Christchurch and Dunedin. In 1955 there were over 6,800 apprentices attending day-release classes or block courses in a wide variety of trades and fifteen years later apprentice training accounted for 41 per cent of the enrolments load of the technical institutes into which some technical schools evolved after 1963. By the mid-1950s, too, industry was demanding that the technical schools turn out technicians trained at a level between that of the tradesmen and that of the university-educated technologist. In 1954 the decision was taken to introduce a special qualification for technicians, the New Zealand Certificate, and preliminary courses in engineering were offered in a number of technical schools the following year. In 1960 the Technicians Certification Authority was established; in that year twenty-nine New Zealand Certificates were awarded. A decade later the number had risen to 590 and 42 per cent of institute enrolments were in technician studies.

The introduction of technician training underlined the need for more advanced technical education facilities as the Director of Education, C. E. Beeby, addressing the Senate of the University of New Zealand admitted. 'A conglomerate type of institution catering for twelve-year-olds and adults, and teaching everything from spelling to professional engineering, has served the country well, but we can scarcely expect it to meet the more complex needs of the future', he said (Currie and Beeby, 1956, 38).

The re-organization of technical education began in 1960 when a large metropolitan technical school was split into a secondary school and a 'technical institute'. During the next ten to fifteen years, technical education was transferred from the secondary to the tertiary sector of the educational system and technical high schools, as such, ceased to exist.

The institutes became responsible for all part-time trade courses and all senior technical work other than that already undertaken by professional schools attached to the universities. By 1972 there were twelve technical institutes with enrolments totalling more than 100,000. Of these, two, the Central Institute of Technology and the Technical Correspondence Institute, had been designated national, and the others, regional, institutes, although in some cases they teach courses for which they recruit nationally.

A special feature of the Central Institute of Technology has, since 1960, been that it provides national courses in areas like chiropody and pharmacy so small or so specialized that the teaching of them can only be justified at one institute in New Zealand. It also gives, through block courses, practical training for students of the Technical Correspondence Institute which teaches almost any course or subject offered anywhere in the state technical system, and for any student, no matter where he may live. Included in its offerings are such subjects as farm forestry, casein-making, boilerhouse practice, fibrous plastering and watch-making.

While the major preoccupation of the regional institutes has traditionally been with trade education, their responsibilities for technician training are mounting. The varied nature of their courses is matched by the diversity of students' qualifications. These range from the two years' secondary schooling required for an apprenticeship to the one or two years in the sixth and seventh forms need for admission to certain full-time courses, some of which extend over three years. Regional institutes are encouraged by the Department of Education to develop programmes particularly suited to area interests and requirements. The indications are that not only will the numbers of such courses increase sharply but that they will become even more varied as the Vocational Training Council and its some twenty-five associated industry training boards help employer and employee groups to identify their training and educational needs (Renwick, 1973, 5). Among courses so far added are occupational therapy, physiotherapy, industrial design and nursing. In 1973, looking to the institutes' own needs, the Central Institute set up a Tutor Training Unit. But while the controlling authorities of institutes have considerable autonomy in deciding course offerings, the Department of Education, to ensure what in its view is 'the balanced, orderly and economical development of technical education as a whole', requires that it approve all proposed courses.

In a country characterized by small settlements strung out over long distances, the problems of providing technical education in provincial centres and rural communities are considerable. For many years local secondary schools have offered a limited range of evening classes, often of a non-vocational hobby class nature but sometimes, depending on proximity to an institute and local traditions, including courses that prepare for trades, technician and professional examinations. In 1969 the government announced that technical education in the larger centres was to be upgraded. Separate 'area institutes' can now be established if there is work for ten full-time teachers. Four were established by 1972.

During the 1960s technical and vocational education had come of age as former secondary school 'night techs' blossomed into tertiary level institutes enrolling growing numbers of full-time, as well as part-time students, many of them in advanced courses. The technical institute was no longer, as the assistant-director general remarked in his opening address to the Technical Institutes' Association 1972 Conference, 'the poor relation from the wrong side of the educational tracks'. Its future had come alive with challenging possibilities.

The universities

In 1945 internal university enrolments totalled 8,000 and there were 640 graduates of the University of New Zealand at the first degree level and 125 at the post graduate level. In 1970 the number of internal students had quadrupled and the six autonomous universities graduated 3,451 students at the first degree level and 846 at the post-graduate. The most marked increase in enrolments was from about 1956 on after a temporary fall in the early 1950s caused by the lower birth-rate of the depression period. Between 1960 and 1970 student numbers doubled and the percentage of full-time students rose from 54 to 73, a trend accelerated after 1962 by a more generous government bursary and boarding allowances scheme intended to reward success and penalize failure. By the end of the 1960s the proportion of the eighteen- to twenty-four-year-old age group attending university in New Zealand was almost double that in Great Britain although still only a fifth of that in the United States of America. Inevitably, national spending of universities soared; in 1937–8 it was 2·8 per cent of the Education Vote and in 1967–8 it was 21 per cent.

Improvement 1959-69			% Increase ↓
Student roll	14 000	30 000	120
Full time	54%	72%	
Degrees and diplomas	1 521	5 173	240
1st degrees	1 012	3 451	241
Diplomas	285	661	132
Honours	147	826	462
Post-graduate degrees	197	846	328
Post-graduate diplomas	27	216	700
Doctorates	11	79	618

Figure 5   Attainment at university, 1959–69
              (Source: Department of Education)

The universities managed, during a decade of unprecedented increases in the number of qualified school leavers, to avoid the practice quite common abroad of offering a fixed number of places. (Only in two professional schools, medicine and veterinary science, is entry competitive and the intake controlled in what the government considers the national interest.) The 'open' policy of the universities allows provisional admission to be granted to applicants over twenty-one who lack the formal qualifications; unmatriculated students may be admitted to certain undergraduate courses and provision has always been made for part-timers. Massey University at Palmerston North has, since 1961–2, undertaken national responsibility for extramural studies. Courses for the 2,000 or so extramural students, many of them teachers, closely parallel those for internal students. Written work is required at intervals throughout the academic year and attendance at vacation courses is sometimes mandatory. A degree cannot be completed by extramural study alone. In all the universities, students not making reasonable academic progress may be excluded, subject to an elaborate appellate procedure.

There are no 'prestige' universities in New Zealand, a student's choice of a university being largely determined by the course he wishes to take and the availability of lodgings. It is not uncommon to begin degree work in one university and complete it at another.

New Zealand universities have always been teaching rather than research institutions, the content and presentation of courses being the responsibility of semi-autonomous subject departments. Only at the University of Waikato, where schools of studies replaced departments and faculties, has a systematic attempt been made to break down the characteristic narrow departmentalism. But the Waikato contextual approach to university education did not sit easily alongside the unit system and a more conventional pattern had to be substituted. The members of the Academic Advisory Committee to the University Grants Committee, who apparently hoped to create in Waikato an Antipodean Sussex, failed to take sufficient account of the traditional assumptions and expectations of university education held by the general public and not a few educators and students. Nevertheless, more attempts to break down departmentalism are overdue. The quality of teaching and learning might be much improved in all the universities if the departments were to sacrifice some of their present autonomy and collaborate more closely in cross-disciplinary teaching and research. Less reliance on the traditional lecture would also help.

The emphasis on teaching has been reduced since the government, on the recommendation of the 1959 Committee on New Zealand Universities, whose report was a turning point in university development, substantially increased money available for research and in 1964 introduced a new concept in post-graduate scholarships intended to encourage post-graduate study. In 1970 the government further increased research possibilities by the decision to equip all the universities with better computer facilities. But already the fear was being expressed that the pendulum had swung too far and that there was too much research in institutions whose major responsibility must continue to be to provide well designed and well taught courses (Bates, ed., 1970).

From 1927 until the end of the 1960s when degree patterns in all universities began to change, first degrees in Arts and Science consisted of 'units'—nine and eight respectively—which could be accumulated piecemeal and often rather haphazardly over a number of years. (A 'unit' was one year's work in a subject usually followed by an examination involving at least two papers.) In first degrees candidates had normally to pass a prescribed minimum number of subjects at the first, second and third stages to satisfy degree requirements. Consequently a New Zealand bachelor's degree seldom represented a deep, coherent and systematic training in a discipline although, as demands grew, so did student performance. Only the small number of students who took an honours degree involving one or two years of specialized study beyond the first degree, worked in one subject area in a concentrated and intensive way.

An unfortunate feature of the New Zealand first degree structure has been that it contributes to the high failure rates among students in many faculties. In the British universities, where the majority of students graduate in the minimum time, undergraduates are examined on their year's work as a whole or even over longer periods. But in New Zealand each unit or paper has to be passed separately, thus maximizing the possibility of failure among first degree students. This is already high because some 25 per cent of them still attend part-time (compared with 3 per cent in Great Britain), because New Zealand students are comparatively young and because most have to supplement their state bursaries by taking non-academic vacation work. There is no doubt that New Zealand universities could achieve a graduation rate similar to that in Britain but only at a price which few New Zealanders would want to pay: a substantial raising of the entry standards; the abandonment of part-time study and a doubling or trebling of the expenditure on each student. 'A failure rate higher than the British (though not obviously higher than that of more comparable universities) is the tax levied upon New Zealanders for having the kind of universities which they have evolved over the years and which they appear to prefer' (Conference of Universities, 1969, 50).

The single, most critical, problem which faced the New Zealand universities from 1945 to 1970 was their inability to recruit qualified staff when tertiary education was expanding throughout the western world. Better conditions and markedly more generous salary scales in the United Kingdom and Australia, pre-war the two most fruitful recruitment fields, sharply reduced the number of high quality academics interested in coming to New Zealand. Each university faced the same dilemma: how to keep subjects going without making poor appointments. The consequences of preferring quality were underlined by the Committee on New Zealand Universities. 'At the University of Canterbury', it reported, 'we were informed that the 687 students enrolled for courses in mathematics had six full-time teachers to guide them; and 462 students of education were served by five full-time members of staff' (Committee on New Zealand Universities, 1959, 57). After the implementation of the committee's salary recommendations the universities had some success in attracting staff from overseas, often their own former graduates, and staff to student ratios improved. At the Victoria University of Wellington, for example, it fell from 1 to 18·8 in 1959 to 1 to 12·5 ten years later. Difficulties in recruiting almost disappeared in 1971 as a result of the slowing down of university expansion in North America and Great Britain.

Overseas students

Although in time the existence of the University of the South Pacific, which began degree courses in 1969, must reduce the numbers of students coming to New Zealand from the Pacific territories, it cannot be expected, immediately, to meet all the demands and needs of the region for higher education. Meantime, it is probable that large numbers of students, private as well as sponsored, will continue to seek admission to New Zealand universities. In 1970, for instance, 622 private students came from Fiji alone.

The growing numbers of private students from overseas entering New Zealand universities (apart from a group of senior secondary pupils, most overseas students are undergraduates) began, in the late 1960s, to cause concern in university and government circles. The influx resulted from the fact that it is easier, academically, for over-seas students to enter New Zealand universities than Australian and also that tuition fees are lower in New Zealand than in almost any other English-speaking country. Although the education of private overseas students has always been regarded as part of New Zealand's official aid programme—by 1970 the New Zealand taxpayer was contributing more towards the cost of the education of the 3,400 private students in the country's schools and universities than he was towards that of its 1,250 sponsored students—the 49 per cent increase in the numbers of private overseas students at New Zealand universities which occurred in 1969–70 convinced the universities and the government that the time had come to control admission more rigorously. Late in 1970 legislation was passed, the intention of which was to ensure that overseas students were not more than about 7 per cent of the total roll of internal university students. (In Great Britain the percentage is over 9.) The imposition of an additional form of restraint, higher fees for overseas students, was also discussed although a final decision was not reached. Spokes-men for the New Zealand University Students' Association vigor-ously opposed such discriminatory treatment. Morals aside, it is possible, however, that even though most private students are from wealthy families, less generous treatment of them might not be to the eventual advantage of New Zealand in terms of diplomatic relations and access to export markets.

Universities and the community

The spectacular university expansion between 1960 and 1970 led to an unusual measure of public discussion. For a time there was wide-ranging criticism of the universities, much of it stemming from two causes: their apparently voracious consumption of public money and the alleged high failure rate among their students.

In his 1967 Budget speech, the Minister of Finance deliberately drew attention to the growing cost of higher education. He said (*NZPD*, 1967, vol. 351, 1271–2):

> In recent years expenditure has increased much more rapidly in the university field than in other areas of education. . . . The upsurge in spending on university education points to the need

for some reappraisal of the allocation of scarce resources of money and personnel to ensure that they are being expended in the manner most beneficial to the New Zealand people.

Early in 1969 he issued a warning that the time would come 'in the foreseeable future' when the demands of the universities for money would be so great that a Minister of Finance in some government would have to say, 'Stop, I cannot finance this' (Volkerling, ed., 1969, 13).

The minister's concern was shared by the many New Zealanders who have long regarded the universities with a degree of suspicion. Unfortunately for the universities the minister's remarks coincided with the publication of a report by the Director of the New Zealand Council for Educational Research on the success and failure of their first year students (Parkyn, 1967). This appeared to suggest that the wastage rate through failures was excessively high in New Zealand. The fact that the data were ten years old by the time the report was published was conveniently ignored by the critics who wished to belabour the universities. At the request of the Minister of Finance, a Treasury official attempted to calculate what these failures were costing the country each year. He arrived at the staggering figure of $10 million. While the accuracy—indeed, the very feasibility—of this kind of calculation was immediately challenged (it was perfunctorily dismissed by one senior university man as having an Alice in Wonderland air of unreality about it), the Minister of Finance remained adamant that, in his opinion, it was a reasonably accurate measure in monetary terms of the degree of waste caused annually by the high university failure rates (Volkerling, ed., 1969, 17).

The implication was clear; in the not-too-distant future the universities might be forced to reconsider their practice of admitting all who, having reached the minimum—and not very exacting—entrance standard wished to matriculate. The minister did not threaten direct government action; he merely reminded the universities, shrewdly using the words of Sir Eric Ashby of the University Grants Committee in the United Kingdom, that 'opportunities for influence by the Government occur once in every five years when the quinquennial grant is announced, and from time to time during the quinquennium when capital expenditure grants are decided upon, or when increases in salaries are announced' (Volkerling, ed., 1969, 12). University spokesmen refused to be drawn into discussing the wisdom of retaining open entry to the universities. They argued that it was not for the universities alone to decide entrance policy. Policy ultimately depended on the amount of money the government was prepared to spend on higher education. If finance was inadequate, the universities would be forced to decide whether to allow standards generally in the universities to decline, or to restrict entry.

The debate initiated by the Minister of Finance was cut short by the Minister of Education who declared that it would remain government policy to make places available for all who, having qualified, wished to enter a university. This forthright statement indicated that he and the majority of his cabinet colleagues realized that no government in New Zealand will ever be able, lightly, to depart from the established policy of open entry. Any restriction on entry severe enough to reduce appreciably the cost of higher education would antagonize a great many people. And when more, not fewer graduates are needed, a restricted entry policy would perhaps reduce the number of men and women graduates, because among those refused entry would be about 'as many potential passers as failures' (Parkyn, 1967, 4). The universities have no great desire to restrict entry. On the contrary most university teachers would prefer to see existing exclusion regulations employed with greater vigour against those students who, once admitted, fail to make satisfactory progress towards a degree.

However, the open entry policy was not the root cause of the threatened crisis in university expenditure in the 1960s. The real reason was the woeful neglect of university needs, actual and potential, from 1945 to 1960. The Hughes Parry committee described the New Zealand attitude to universities as typical of a country not far removed from a pioneer tradition where there is always a willingness to cater for today and tomorrow but where planning too far ahead is viewed with grave suspicion. Practice without theory is preferred (Committee on New Zealand Universities, 1959, 8). As a result, in New Zealand, government spending on the universities tends to be always too little, too late.

Certain sections of the public believe that government spending on the universities should be related in some undefined way to the immediate benefits the universities can provide in terms of technological discoveries, of work skills, scientific discoveries of economic value, or contributions towards solving the community's day-to-day problems. Higher education, it is argued, should have more 'relevance'. University spokesmen, while not denying that their institutions have some civic and social obligations, refuse to accept that they are community service stations or that a university education should be regarded as an economic investment on which interest can be expected. There is not only an important place in universities for studies not specifically vocational but there is also a place for fundamental research which might or might not be of direct material value. Nevertheless, the universities, while reluctant to yield to the blandishments of industrialists and the business community and open their doors to all manner of technical subjects, are very aware that what the Vice-Chancellor of the University of New Zealand pointed out in 1956 remains true: if the universities gather their academic skirts around them and retreat to the pleasant 'Groves of Academe' where only the purest of pure academic subjects are offered to an intellectual élite, they will almost certainly wilt and die in the New Zealand environment (Currie and Beeby, 1956).

University–technical institute relationships

Although the technical institutes are an integral and evolving part of the tertiary education structure, their particular functions have never been defined exactly and this lack of definition is now creating difficulties for the universities upon whose domain the technical institutes appear to be encroaching. The universities believe it is in their own and the country's interests to avoid such wasteful duplication. They are anxious that the advice given by a former Director of Education in 1956 should still be heeded. 'Every precaution', Dr C. E. Beeby warned the University of New Zealand Senate, 'should be taken to prevent the universities' claims for legitimate expansion being prejudiced by a new enthusiasm for technical education. . . . The country needs the products of both the university and the technical colleges. . . . If one type of institution is developed at the expense of the other, both will, in the long run, suffer' (Currie and Beeby, 1956, 54).

General oversight of the orderly development of tertiary education is the responsibility of the Department of Education and the

University Grants Committee but until 1972 there was no formal machinery which brought together in a committee representatives of the administrative, statutory, advisory and controlling authorities directly concerned with relationships between universities and technical institutes.

At the local level, however, there was informal consultation and co-operation. For example, arrangements were worked out to permit work done in one kind of institution to be credited towards a qualification in the other. The University Schools of Engineering in Auckland and Canterbury allow students who have gained, with distinction, a New Zealand Certificate in Engineering, one and two years' credit respectively towards their bachelors' degrees. Although only about one-third of the technicians thus qualifying take advantage of this concession, the majority of those who do complete their degrees in the minimum time. Cross-crediting of this kind, however, has the disadvantage that it further accentuates the difficulty New Zealand industry has of securing a satisfactory ratio between technicians and graduates. In engineering, for example, where the ideal ratio is reckoned to be two or three technicians to one graduate, the ratio of technicians to graduates completing their qualifications in 1967 was only 0·93 to 1.

Most transfers take place from the technical institutes to the universities. Movement the other way is uncommon. The institutes do not encourage students who have failed at university to change over to the technical institutes. Experience has shown that such students are just as likely to fail in the second institution. They are conditioned to failure, disorganized in their approach to their studies and often ill at ease among their more highly motivated fellow students (Bates, ed., 1970, 134–43). Had these students gone to a technical institute in the first place they might have done well. The Department of Education and the separate institutes must do more to inform teachers, parents and pupils about courses available and the career opportunities they open up. Increases in technical institute bursaries and boarding allowances announced in 1971 and 1972, improved health services, better student union and library facilities and the provision of halls of residence should convince the technical student that he, like his institution, is no longer tertiary education's poor relation.

The Department of Education expects the number of full-time

technical institute students to increase sharply and the rate of growth of the institutes to be greater than that of the universities. Its roll projections for the 1970s give an estimated increase of 71 per cent for universities and 90 per cent for institutes. As demand grows and new courses are pioneered, the question arises as to what academic awards the institutes should be authorized to confer. Should New Zealand establish the equivalent of the British Council for National Academic Awards? There were indications in the late 1960s that the government favoured a binary system. In 1968 the Minister of Education spoke of the likelihood that the Central Institute of Technology would become 'virtually a technical university' (*NZPD*, 1968, vol. 356, 996). How closely the minister's views and those of his senior departmental advisers coincided cannot be judged. Later departmental statements have implied that teaching to degree level is not yet favoured (Renwick, 1973, 5-6). A final answer to the question may be delayed until after the Central Institute is established on its new 40-acre site at Heretaunga in 1973 when, its principal has promised, 'it will no longer be necessary for students to transfer to another system of education to obtain their highest qualifications' (*Evening Post*, 26 February 1969).

The emphasis at the new institute is to be entirely on advanced training. Trade courses and part-time evening and day-release classes, traditionally the mainstay of technical institutes, will be left to the regional institutes. All local responsibilities will be shed and the concentration will be on national courses which will not then be available anywhere else. Halls of residence with accommodation for 500 students will be built in the vicinity.

These plans have had a mixed reception. No one questioned the wisdom of high-level national courses where student demand was limited, expensive equipment needed, or appropriate staff in short supply. Regional institute spokesmen, however, expressed concern that all such courses were to be concentrated at the Central Institute. They preferred some national courses to be taught locally because a Central Institute monopoly would, it was argued, impoverish regional institutes. Department of Education policy, however, has consistently been to concentrate high-level, specialized courses in the Central Institute, a policy likely, as the Minister of Education predicted in 1968, to create a technological university.

Such a university can only be justified if it can be shown that existing universities have ignored commercial, business and industrial interests, or have pursued a policy of calculated separateness from technical institutes and teachers' colleges. But the New Zealand universities from their beginnings have always responded, like the United States land grant colleges they resemble, to local needs, pressures and demands. They have never been ivory towers. It would seem prudent, therefore, to continue to develop technology as required in existing comprehensive university centres.

University-teachers' college relationships

In 1967 the National Advisory Council on the Training of Teachers invited the universities to consider the part they might wish to play in teacher training. The council's memorandum was an attempt to clarify the heads under which discussion and consultation might usefully take place and began by pointing out that every public inquiry into either university education or the training of teachers this century had considered the contribution the universities should make to teacher training. In 1959 the Committee on New Zealand Universities, for example, recommended that all the universities should assume more responsibility for the professional as well as the general education of primary and secondary teachers, and expressed the hope that an experimental or prototype secondary teacher training programme could be developed in one university in the near future. The Commission on Education two years later, impressed by submissions urging closer liaison between the universities and the teachers' colleges, recommended that the universities, through English-style institutes of education, become formally responsible for all teacher training (Commission on Education, 1962, 500–11).

The proposed institutes came to nothing because they were unnecessarily complicated, costly and ill-suited to New Zealand conditions. Discussion of the commission's recommendations for teacher training, however, kept the whole question of university-teachers' college relations very much to the fore throughout the 1960s. The recommendation of the Committee on Higher Education in Great Britain in 1963 that universities in the United Kingdom should try to devise a distinctive professional degree for teachers was considered carefully in New Zealand but only the University of Waikato, and later Massey University, were willing to introduce a

Bachelor of Education degree incorporating some courses taught at neighbouring teachers' colleges. In the four other universities it was believed first, that such a degree could easily become stigmatized as inferior to established bachelors' degrees and secondly, that a special teachers' degree was unnecessary in New Zealand where, from their inception, the constituent colleges of the federal university had encouraged teachers and teachers' college students to study as part-time or external students. Further, since 1963, opportunities for full-time university study by teachers' college students had been extended by the introduction of more varied and generous bursary and studentship schemes. For these reasons the universities of Auckland, Wellington, Canterbury and Otago rejected the notion of a Bachelor of Education as a first degree. They offered, instead, to introduce new courses catering to the needs of teachers. In the Victoria University of Wellington some degree credit is given for advanced college courses passed with distinction.

While the universities were willing to help in these ways they were reluctant to become directly involved, as the National Advisory Council on Teacher Training had suggested, in the actual training of teachers. The universities, jealous of their academic standards, understandably did not want to be associated too closely with another form of tertiary education which, by rumour and repute, made low scholarly demands upon its students.

But not only university attitudes and traditional practices worked against closer liaison between the universities and the teachers' colleges. The teachers' colleges were as suspicious as the universities. Many college staff, proud of the distinctive character and traditions of their institutions, feared that the price of greater academic respectability would be too high. Resistance also came from the Department of Education which, both directly, and indirectly through the Auckland, South Auckland, Wanganui, Wellington, Canterbury and Otago Education Boards, effectively controlled teacher training. A possible deadlock was averted by the setting up of teachers' college councils on which the universities, as well as other educational interests, are represented. Consequently, university–teachers' college links are now stronger everywhere.

As the teachers' colleges, like the technical institutes, grow in academic stature and establish their claim to educate and train a wider range of professional groups, the possibility of creating one grants committee to oversee the whole field of tertiary education deserves consideration. Such a committee would help promote academic co-operation and ensure the best use of limited resources, intellectual as well as economic.

II

Conclusion

Marked educational progress has been made in New Zealand in the three decades since the then Minister of Education, Peter Fraser, officially declared that 'every person, whatever his level of academic ability, whether he be rich or poor, whether he live in town or country, has a right, as a citizen, to a free education of the kind for which he is best fitted and to the fullest extent of his powers'. The teacher shortage has been largely overcome; the government is committed to reducing the size of both primary and secondary school classes in the early 1970s; a major initiative in providing facilities for the under-fives is promised; three-year primary teacher training is an established fact; the grading system is no longer 'at the very heart of all the evils' of the education system (Campbell, ed., 1938, 478); new schools are better designed and better equipped; steady improvements have taken place in the processes of curriculum development; the introduction of area and Form I–VII schools has not only improved the quality of rural education but has shown that the division between primary and secondary schooling is an anachronistic legacy; everywhere, non-selective, comprehensive secondary schools are trying, with varying success, to teach all children of secondary school age; a national system of tertiary level technical education has evolved; specialist services have been developed and are being extended to help pupils requiring personal, educational or vocational guidance while, in scope and quality, the provision now made for children who are intellectually or physically handicapped or are emotionally disturbed compares not unfavourably with that made in most other countries.

But these advances in equalizing and extending educational opportunities should not blind either the authorities or the public to chronic deficiencies and new shortcomings. The problem of underachievement among Polynesian children, for example, after nearly twenty years of discussion and theorizing, is only now being tackled vigorously and as a matter of urgency.

A much older problem, one that in 1937 Dr William Boyd, the eminent Scottish educationist, called the 'grievous lack of co-ordination' between primary and secondary sub-systems still persists. Educational politics probably make impossible a complete merger of the two services but some attempt at compromise should be tried. Administratively, separate education boards and governing bodies could be brought together in regional boards controlling more than one level of education. The need for a new education board in Northland offers a chance to experiment.

(One in three New Zealanders)

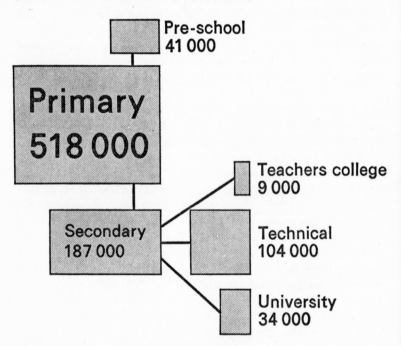

Pre-school 41 000

Primary 518 000

Teachers college 9 000

Secondary 187 000

Technical 104 000

University 34 000

Total=893 000

Figure 6   Roll call, 1970 (Source: Table 4, E.1, 1971; nearest thousand)

All is not well, either, within our secondary schools. Few have avoided alienating significant numbers of their senior pupils. In 1971, the Department of Education implicitly acknowledged the need to begin a fundamental re-thinking of the functions of secondary schools by calling the first of an intended series of curriculum review conferences with the particular purpose of examining the nature and extent of general education. It is clear that the two years of 'core' studies introduced in 1945 are inadequate and the choice now seems to lie between three and four years. There is no suggestion, however, that New Zealand follow the British example and raise the school leaving age to sixteen. Indeed, because the school is not self-evidently the best place for some young people and 'the more they have the worse they may be for it' (Renwick, 1972, 9), there is some support for a proposal made by the Minister of Education in 1973 to abolish both minimum and maximum leaving ages and to allow a pupil either to leave school before fifteen or to compel him to stay beyond that age, the final decision to be made after consultation between pupil, parents, teachers and the school guidance counsellor. Early leavers could be guided towards other kinds of educative experiences for which responsibility could rest with the community colleges which the third Labour Government elected in 1972 proposes to establish to widen the opportunities for continuing education, especially in smaller centres. A final decision on the functions and responsibilities of community colleges will be made after a review of tertiary education instituted in 1973 (*NZPD*, 1973, vol. 382, 614).

Such a review was timely. With the growth in extent and complexity of tertiary education in the 1960s the need for new administrative relationships became clear. The question was asked, for example, whether teachers' colleges should continue to be independent institutions or be merged either with the universities or with technical institutes or even, possibly, community colleges. As long ago as 1937, Dr Isaac Kandel and Dr William Boyd, guest lecturers at a series of regional educational seminars were urging that training colleges be brought under the aegis and influence of the university (Campbell, ed., 1938, 466, 487). The hitherto privileged, but criticized status of the universities, will also be examined in the light of the third Labour Government's determination to extend educational opportunities. 'Universities are important,' the Minister of

Education said, 'but we must never lose sight of the fact that they provide educational opportunities for only about 12 per cent of our school leavers, and the other 88 per cent are also entitled to a fair chance' (*NZPD*, 1973, vol. 382, 614).

It is unlikely that, in educational planning, the new government will be able to adhere unswervingly to its declared social demand policy. As in the late 1960s, many want the return the nation is receiving on its investment in education to be looked at more critically. They believe that a new approach to planning is urgently needed to generate realistic objectives and to avoid distortions within the economy as a whole. In 1968, for the first time in New Zealand, education was included among the terms of reference of an economic survey, the National Development Conference. By so doing, the government tacitly admitted that, besides the planning that can be expected from the periodic and discrete commissions and committees of inquiry which served New Zealand education well in the past, there is need for planning using, for example, the sophisticated techniques of rate of return analysis and systems theory.

The National Development Conference, the grandest of a series of conferences in the 1960s in which New Zealand sought her future in words and some figures, was attended by over 500 businessmen, farmers, public servants and university teachers. The holding of a national economic planning conference in 1968 had been prompted by the cumulative effect of the continuing fall in the price of primary produce, by the stated intention of the British Government to continue negotiations for entry into the European Economic Community and the consequent urgent need to gain access to new markets, and by the long-term economic implications of the post-war baby boom (Franklin, 1969, 2). The purpose of the conference was to plan for economic growth by defining objectives, ordering priorities and stating claims to resources. For the first time an attempt was made to set targets for education in the context of the overall economy.

The Steering Committee of the conference established an Education, Training and Research Committee with fairly specific terms of reference. The committee was asked, for example, to pay 'particular attention to tertiary education and the role of the institutions concerned' (Education, Training and Research Committee, National Development Conference, 1969, 5). This responsibility the committee discharged with great thoroughness, becoming, through the attention it paid to the technical institutes, almost a commission on technical education. Because the universities had been the subject of a major inquiry exactly ten years earlier, the committee attempted only to analyse the relationships, actual and potential, between the universities, the technical institutes and the teachers' colleges. Such comments as the committee did make on the universities were guarded. By concluding that the money spent on the universities was money well spent, it to some degree spiked the guns of those who favoured retrenchment in university spending. Had it not been for the committee's blessing, the quinquennial grant to the universities in 1970 might have been even less generous than it was.

In keeping with the general spirit and approach of the conference, the report of the Education, Training and Research Committee included one feature unique in a New Zealand report on education, a summary forecast, unavoidably somewhat impressionistic, of state expenditure on the education system for the period 1967–8 to 1978–9. Another novel and significant feature of the committee's report was its recommendation that a permanent consultative body, outside the Department of Education and under an independent chairman, be set up to facilitate and promote long-range, continuous, educational planning. The government acted promptly on this recommendation by establishing a permanent, nine-member Advisory Council on Educational Planning, to consider or advise on matters referred to it by the Minister of Education, the Director-General of Education or the National Development Conference.

How independent and influential an advisory and planning agency outside the Department of Education (which set up its own Research and Planning Unit in 1970) can really be, remains to be seen. An earlier attempt to develop an effective independent advisory body was frustrated by the Department of Education in the 1920s. There is a very real danger that any such body, once its initial enthusiasm has been exhausted, will become little more than an additional public relations section of the Department of Education. Certainly, the council has been active since its formation. Working parties have published reports on *University–Technical Institute Relationships* and *Technical and Industrial Academic Awards*; at the Department of Education's request, the Standing Committee on Teacher Training

appointed in 1970 evaluated three proposed university based schemes
for teacher education; in 1972 the council, in conjunction with the
National Commission for UNESCO, organized a seminar on
educational planning with observers and consultants from overseas;
later in the year the council acted as steering committee for a proposed two-stage Educational Priorities Conference called by the
Minister of Education. Intended to involve as many interest groups
as possible in planning, the conference proved too large to be
successful and the Minister of Education in the new Labour
administration cancelled the second session and substituted his own
Development Conference lasting more than a year and involving a
series of regional seminars or public forums in up to fifteen centres.
The Advisory Council was again asked to act as steering committee
and its working parties formed for the original Priorities Conference
were invited to continue preparing discussion papers on aims and
objectives of education, improving learning and teaching, and
organization and administration. It is likely to be the council's
province, after the seminars in 1974, to recommend priorities for
educational development in accordance with the share of the national
economic resources that can realistically be allocated to education
during the next decade. To encourage the department into trying,
and the government into paying for, more flexible and imaginative
approaches to education will demand a rare combination of far-
sightedness, originality and discretion from council members. If the
Advisory Council can resist the common New Zealand failing of
becoming over-dependent on the public servant, if it can fulfil its
primary function of relating education to the economic needs of the
community, if its members prove to be men and women of vision,
it may do much to ensure that the best possible use is made of New
Zealand's single most valuable resource, her people.

Suggestions for further reading

(a) Background

CAMERON, W. J. (1965) *New Zealand*, Englewood Cliffs, N.J., Prentice-Hall (Modern Nations in Historical Perspective Series). An expatriate New Zealander's attempt to isolate the trends and factors that have contributed most significantly to New Zealand's present-day character and problems.

DEPARTMENT OF STATISTICS. *New Zealand Official Yearbook*, Wellington, Government Printer. This annual publication describes the physical resources of the country and their use. It enumerates statistics of the population, their production, their trade and their national finances, their wages and their savings, their housing and food consumption, their means of communication and their international relationships. Supplementary material gives other social, administrative and legislative information.

FORSTER, J. (ed.) (1969) *Social Process in New Zealand*, Auckland, Longman Paul. Readings in sociology, many with direct relevance for the student of the New Zealand educational system.

MCLEOD, A. L. (ed.) (1968) *The Pattern of New Zealand Culture*, Melbourne, Oxford University Press; Ithaca, N.Y., Cornell University Press. An ambitious but uneven book describing contemporary New Zealand and New Zealanders.

MCLINTOCK, A. H. (ed.) (1966) *An Encyclopaedia of New Zealand*, 3 vols, Wellington, Government Printer. Invaluable reference books; the section on education in Volume One is excellent.

METGE, JOAN (1967) *The Maoris of New Zealand*, London, Routledge & Kegan Paul. An introductory study of Maori society and culture, past and present.

OLIVER, W. H. (1963) *The Story of New Zealand*, London, Faber. A scholarly, readable history.

SCHWIMMER, E. (ed.) (1968) *The Maori People in the Sixties*, Auckland, Blackwood & Janet Paul. In this symposium a number of authors pinpoint and try to explain the changes which have taken place among the Maori people since about 1940.

SUTCH, W. B. (rev. edn) (1969) *Poverty and Progress in New Zealand*, Wellington, A. H. & A. W. Reed. A history in which the emphasis is

159

upon the advances made in economic and social welfare in New Zealand. Considerable attention is paid to developments in the post-1945 period.

(b) Education

ASHTON-WARNER, SYLVIA (1963) *Teacher*, London, Secker & Warburg. A New Zealand teacher's experiences in classrooms which included both Maori and Pakeha children. The teaching methods used are described in detail.

BALDOCK, CORA VELLEKOOP (1971) *Vocational Choice and Opportunity*, Christchurch, University of Canterbury. An edited description of the results of an empirical study into children's vocational choice which formed the basis of the author's earlier Ph.D. dissertation.

BARRINGTON, J. M. and BEAGLEHOLE, T. H. (in press) *The Maori School in a Changing Society, An Historical Review*, Wellington, New Zealand Council for Educational Research. An amalgam of two master's theses, one in History the other in Education, describing European efforts, from the earliest days of missionary endeavour, to provide formal schooling for Maori children.

BENDER, B. W. (1971) *Linguistic Factors in Maori Education*, Wellington, New Zealand Council for Educational Research. This report contains recommendations for further research into the language difficulties which appear to prevent many Maori children from obtaining full benefit from their schooling.

BRAY, D. H. and HILL, C. G. N. (eds) (1973) *Polynesian and Pakeha in New Zealand Education*, 2 vols, Auckland, Heinemann Educational Books. Appropriate education for Maoris and immigrant Polynesians in New Zealand is examined in the light of their cultures, behavioural characteristics, health and position, past and present, in New Zealand society. In volume I, *The Sharing of Cultures*, the contributions concentrate on general relationships of education to culture and society and in volume II, *Ethnic Difference and the School*, more specifically on schooling and health.

CAMPBELL, A. E., PARKYN, G. W. and EWING, J. L. (rev. edn) (1972) *Compulsory Education in New Zealand*, Paris, UNESCO. A succinct, accurate and up-to-date general survey of the New Zealand school system from its provincial beginnings to the present day.

ELLEY, W. B. and LIVINGSTONE, I. D. (1972) *External Examinations and Internal Assessments*, Wellington, New Zealand Council for Educational Research. Information about New Zealand secondary school examinations brought together in a monograph with suggested alternative paths reform might follow.

EWING, J. L. and SHALLCRASS, J. J. (eds) (1970) *An Introduction to Maori Education: Selected Readings*, Wellington, New Zealand University Press. Articles describing aspects of Maori education, historical and contemporary.

GARDNER, W. J., BEARDSLEY, E. T. and CARTER, T. E. (1973) *A History of the University of Canterbury 1873–1973*, Christchurch, University of Canterbury. About one university whose history epitomizes that of all four older foundations.

HALL, D. O. W. (1970) *New Zealand Adult Education*, London, Michael Joseph. A volume in the series, 'Leeds Studies in Adult Education', this particular book covers the history of adult education in New Zealand from early colonial days to the present.

HAVILL, S. J. and MITCHELL, D. R. (eds) (1972) *Issues in New Zealand Special Education*, Auckland, Hodder & Stoughton. Self-contained papers varying in their critical perceptiveness gathered under the umbrella of Special Education. Each paper touches on historical development, present provision and current issues.

INGLE, S. J. (in press) *Politics of Control: Direction in the New Zealand Education System*, Wellington, New Zealand Council for Educational Research. An edited version of the author's Ph.D. thesis, 'The Politics of Education', an important pioneering study of education interest groups in New Zealand.

MCKENZIE, M. B. (compiler) (1970) *Maori Education 1960–1969: a Bibliography*, Wellington, New Zealand Council for Educational Research.

MACKEY, J. (1967) *The Making of a State Education System*, London, Geoffrey Chapman. Provincial events and experiences which led to the passing of the New Zealand Education Act of 1877 carefully analysed.

MINOGUE, W. J. D. (1971) *Hawaiian and New Zealand Teacher Education*, Wellington, New Zealand Educational Institute. A comparative study up to 1967 following the model proposed by G. Z. F. Bereday in *Comparative Method in Education*.

MITCHELL, F. W. (ed.) (1971) *Looking Ahead in New Zealand Education*, Wellington, A. H. & A. W. Reed. Addresses given at a conference of the New Zealand College of Education, the theme of which was educational planning.

NEW ZEALAND DEPARTMENT OF EDUCATION (1971) *Maori Children and the Teacher*, Wellington, School Publications Branch. A manual to help teachers, particularly newcomers to the profession, assess the backgrounds of Maori pupils who come into their care.

NEW ZEALAND DEPARTMENT OF EDUCATION (1972) *Public Education in 1972*, Wellington, Department of Education. Prepared for a government-called Education Priorities Conference, this bulletin catalogues achievements of the 1960s and hints at plans for the 1970s. It is as full of facts and figures as it is of cautious predictions.

RICHARDSON, E. S. (2nd edn) (1972) *In the Early World*, Wellington, New Zealand Council for Educational Research. The 'success story' of a teacher in a remote country school who was determined to give his pupils a creative education. Well illustrated with examples of the children's work.

RITCHIE, JANE and JAMES (1970) *Child Rearing Patterns in New Zealand*, Wellington, A. H. & A. W. Reed. An easily read analysis of a little recorded aspect of New Zealand society based on interviews over a two-year period with the mothers of 151 four-year-olds.

ROTH, H. O. (1964) *A Bibliography of New Zealand Education*, Wellington, New Zealand Council for Educational Research.

WEBB, L. C. (1937) *The Control of Education in New Zealand*, Wellington, New Zealand Council for Educational Research. A detailed study by a political scientist of evolving administrative arrangements in education in the sixty years following the passage of the 1877 Education Act.

WINTERBOURN, R. (rev. edn) (1971) *Caring for Intellectually Handicapped Children*, Wellington, New Zealand Council for Educational Research. This is the third and substantially revised edition of a manual for parents originally published in 1958.

Bibliography

ALGIE, R. M. (1950) 'Statement', *National Education*, vol. 32, no. 341, 4–5.

ASSOCIATION OF UNIVERSITY TEACHERS (1970) *Trends and Issues in Higher Education*, Wellington, New Zealand Council for Educational Research.

AUSUBEL, D. P. (1958) 'A professional approach to educational problems', *New Zealand Post-Primary Teachers' Association Journal*, vol. 4, no. 5, 12–13.

AUSUBEL, D. P. (1960) *The Fern and the Tiki*, Sydney, Angus & Robertson.

AUSUBEL, D. P. (1961) *Maori Youth*, Wellington, Price Milburn.

BARHAM, I. H. (1965) *English Vocabulary and Sentence Structure of Maori Children*, Wellington, New Zealand Council for Educational Research.

BARON, G. (1965) *Society, Schools and Progress in England*, Oxford, Pergamon Press.

BATES, R. J. (ed.) (1970) *Prospects in New Zealand Education*, Auckland, Hodder & Stoughton.

BAUCKE, W. (1928) *Where the White Man Treads*, Auckland, Wilson & Horton.

BEEBY, C. E. (1938) *The Intermediate Schools of New Zealand*, Wellington, New Zealand Council for Educational Research.

BEEBY, C. E. (1956) 'Administration as an art', *New Zealand Journal of Public Administration*, vol. 18, no. 2, 3–14.

BOAG, P. (1970) 'New Disciplinary Regulations', *New Zealand Post-Primary Teachers' Association Journal*, vol. 17, no. 2, 14–16.

BOYLE, E., CROSLAND, A., and KOGAN, M. (1971) *The Politics of Education*, Harmondsworth, Penguin Books.

BREWARD, I. (1967) *Godless Schools? A Study in Protestant Reactions to the Education Act of 1877*, Christchurch, Presbyterian Bookroom.

BUTCHERS, A. G. (1932) *The Education System*, Auckland, National Printing Co.

BUTTERWORTH, RUTH (1968) 'New Zealand education: progress in a political vacuum', *Extension Course Lectures*, Auckland, Headmasters' Association.

CAMPBELL, A. E. (ed.) (1938) *Modern Trends in Education*, Wellington, Whitcombe & Tombs.

CAMPBELL, A. E. (1941) *Educating New Zealand*, Wellington, Department of Internal Affairs.

163

CAMPBELL, A. E. (1957) 'Address to primary teachers refresher course at Timaru', *Education*, vol. 6, no. 2, 9.

CAMPBELL, A. E. (1960) 'A brief review of recent educational developments in New Zealand' (cyclostyled), submission no. 3 of the Department of Education to the Commission on Education in New Zealand.

CHAPMAN, R. M., JACKSON, W. K., and MITCHELL, A. V. (1962) *New Zealand Politics in Action*, London, Oxford University Press.

COMMITTEE ON NEW ZEALAND UNIVERSITIES (1959) *Report*, Wellington, Government Printer (Chairman: Sir David Hughes Parry).

CONFERENCE OF UNIVERSITIES, VICTORIA UNIVERSITY OF WELLINGTON (1969) 'Papers' (duplicated).

CONGALTON, A. A. and HAVIGHURST, R. J. (1954) 'Status ranking of occupations in New Zealand', *Australian Journal of Psychology*, vol. 6, no. 1, 10–15.

CURRIE, G. A. and BEEBY, C. E. (1956) *Training for Technology in New Zealand*, Wellington, Whitcombe & Tombs.

Dominion (Wellington).

Evening Post (Wellington).

EWING, J. L. (1970) *Development of the New Zealand Primary School Curriculum 1877–1970*, Wellington, New Zealand Council for Educational Research.

FRANKLIN, S. H. (1969) 'The search for new directions', *Pacific Viewpoint*, vol. 10, no. 1, 1–5.

Gisborne Herald (Gisborne).

GOODWIN, J. W. (1962) 'Act now for the future', *National Education*, vol. 44, no. 479, 337–8.

GREAT BRITAIN COMMITTEE ON HIGHER EDUCATION (1963) *Report*, HMSO (Chairman: Lord Robbins).

HAWKINS, H. H. (1960) 'The status of teachers', *National Education*, vol. 42, no. 455, 208–14.

HOLMES, B. (1967) *Problems of Education*, London, Routledge & Kegan Paul.

HUNN, J. K. (1960) *Report on Department of Maori Affairs*, Wellington, Government Printer.

INGLE, S. J. (1967) 'The politics of education', unpublished Ph.D. thesis, the Victoria University of Wellington.

JACKMAN, R. H. (1969) 'Secondary school staffing', *Delta Five*, August, 23–33.

JACKSON, P. M. (ed.) (1931) *Maori and Education*, Wellington, Ferguson & Osborn.

KANDEL, I. L. (1937) *Impressions of Education in New Zealand*, Wellington, New Zealand Council for Educational Research.

Bibliography

KANDEL, I. L. (1938) *Types of Administration*, Melbourne University Press.

LEESE, J. (1950) *Personalities and Power in English Education*, London, E. Arnold.

MAORI EDUCATION FOUNDATION (1965) *Third Annual Report*, Wellington, Government Printer.

MCQUEEN, H. C. (1945) *Vocations for Maori Youth*, Wellington, New Zealand Council for Educational Research.

MASON, H. G. R. (1945) *Education, Today and Tomorrow*, Wellington, Government Printer.

MEIKLE, P. (1961) *School and Nation*, Wellington, New Zealand Council for Educational Research.

MITCHELL, F. W. (ed.) (1968) *New Zealand Education Today*, Wellington, A. H. & A. W. Reed.

MURDOCH, J. H. (1943) *The High Schools of New Zealand*, Wellington, New Zealand Council for Educational Research.

NATIONAL DEVELOPMENT CONFERENCE (1969) *Report of Education, Training and Research Committee*, Wellington, Government Printer.

NEW ZEALAND COMMISSION ON EDUCATION (1962) *Report*, Wellington, Government Printer (Chairman: Sir George Currie).

NEW ZEALAND DEPARTMENT OF EDUCATION *New Zealand Education Gazette*, Wellington, Government Printer.

NEW ZEALAND DEPARTMENT OF EDUCATION (1959) *Post-Primary School Curriculum*, Wellington, Government Printer.

NEW ZEALAND DEPARTMENT OF EDUCATION (1972) *Public Education in 1972*, Wellington, Department of Education.

NEW ZEALAND DEPARTMENT OF EDUCATION (1971) *Report of the Committee of Inquiry into Pre-School Education*, Wellington, Government Printer (Chairman: Professor C. G. Hill).

NEW ZEALAND DEPARTMENT OF EDUCATION, CURRICULUM DEVELOPMENT UNIT (1972) *The Secondary School Curriculum: 5*, Wellington, Department of Education.

NEW ZEALAND DEPARTMENT OF EDUCATION, PUBLIC RELATIONS SECTION (1968) *Education in New Zealand*, Wellington, Department of Education.

NEW ZEALAND EDUCATIONAL INSTITUTE (1967) *Report and Recommendations on Maori Education*, Wellington, Educational Institute.

NEW ZEALAND EDUCATIONAL INSTITUTE (1968) *Report of Annual Meeting*, Wellington, Educational Institute.

New Zealand Herald (Auckland).

NEW ZEALAND PARLIAMENT. HOUSE OF REPRESENTATIVES. *Appendices to the Journals (A to J)*, Wellington, Government Printer.

NEW ZEALAND PARLIAMENT. HOUSE OF REPRESENTATIVES. *Debates, (NZPD)*

Wellington, Government Printer.

NEW ZEALAND PARLIAMENT. PUBLIC EXPENDITURE COMMITTEE (1966) *Report*, Wellington, Government Printer (Chairman: Mr R. D. Muldoon).

NEW ZEALAND UNIVERSITIES STUDENTS' ASSOCIATION (1969) 'Notes on the University Grants Committee' (cyclostyled).

NGATA, A. (1893) *The Past and the Future of the Maori*, Christchurch Press Company.

PARKYN, G. W. (1967) *Success and Failure at the University*, vol. 2, Wellington, New Zealand Council for Educational Research.

RAMSAY, P. D. K. (1969) 'Planning, policy and practice in Maori education, 1936–1968', unpublished M.A. thesis, the Victoria University of Wellington.

RENWICK, W. L. (1970) 'Educational planning in New Zealand' (cyclostyled).

RENWICK, W. L. (1972) *New Tasks for Secondary Education*, Wellington, Curriculum Development Unit, Department of Education.

RENWICK, W. L. (1973) 'Entering a new phase', *Education*, vol. 22, no. 3, 3–8.

RITCHIE, J. (1963) *The Making of a Maori*, Wellington, A. H. & A. W. Reed.

ROBERTS, J. L. (ed.) (1961) *Decentralisation in New Zealand Government Administration*, London, Oxford University Press.

ROSS, A. (ed.) (1969) *New Zealand's Record in the Pacific Islands in the Twentieth Century*, Auckland, Longman Paul.

SCHWIMMER, E. (1962) 'The Maori Education Foundation', *Comment*, vol. 3, no. 4, 7–11.

SMITH, L. (1958) 'An Investigation into the Influence of Reading Achievement in English on Intelligence Test Performances of Maori Children', unpublished M.A. thesis, University of Auckland.

SUPERVISOR, CORRESPONDENCE SCHOOL DIPLOMA IN TEACHING DIVISION (1966) 'Report to the Director-General of Education' (typewritten).

VELLEKOOP, C. (1968) 'Social stratification in New Zealand', unpublished Ph.D. thesis, University of Canterbury.

VOLKERLING, M. (ed.) (1969) *The Politics of Education*, Auckland University Students' Association.

WATSON, J. E. (1964) *Intermediate Schooling in New Zealand*, Wellington, New Zealand Council for Educational Research.

WATSON, J. E. (1967) *Horizons of Unknown Power*, Wellington, New Zealand Council for Educational Research.

Index